#nyc

Kyle Warren

BROADWAY PLAY PUBLISHING INC
New York
www.broadwayplaypublishing.com
info@broadwayplaypublishing.com

#nyc

© Copyright 2017 Kyle Warren

Cover art by Ian Epstein

First edition: July 2017
I S B N: 978-0-88145-727-8

Book design: Marie Donovan
Page make-up: Adobe InDesign
Typeface: Palatino

Originally commissioned, developed and produced by UglyRhino Productions.

Developed at the Lark Play Development Center, New York City.

CHARACTERS & SETTING

OLIVER JUDD, *late thirties, a former estate lawyer and* DENISE's *husband*

TRACY HOLSTEIN, *late twenties, a newspaper journalist engaged to* TODD

TODD, *28, a middle school Algebra teacher engaged to* TRACY

JOHN KENDRICK, *early seventies, the Mayor of New York City*

DENISE POWELL, *late thirties, First Deputy Mayor of New York City,* OLIVER's *wife*

HELEN, *late sixties, a lifetime Upper East Side resident and* TODD's *mother*

The actor playing HELEN *also plays* FIRST INTERROGATOR

The actor playing TRACY *also plays* SECOND INTERROGATOR

The actor playing DENISE *also plays* THIRD INTERROGATOR

The actor playing TODD *also plays* FOURTH INTERROGATOR

Place: New York City
Time: Now, or thereabouts

Throughout the play, some dialogue and scenes should overlap. Slashes in dialogue indicate when the following line should begin. Lines and segments of scenes designated "overlap with above/below" should be read concurrently.

"Time alone reveals the virtue of a man,
but his evil can be gathered in a single day."
Sophocles, *Oedipus Rex*

A Prologue

Monday, July 6

(A single sheet of paper drifts down onto a New York City sidewalk. It lands at the feet of TRACY HOLSTEIN *who is smoking a cigarette and checking Twitter on her cell phone. Barely taking her eyes off the screen to pick up the paper, she notices a typed passage. She lets the phone fall to her side as she begins to read.)*

TRACY: "A Prologue."

(Elsewhere, OLIVER JUDD *recites the prologue to his book.)*

OLIVER: A Prologue.
The first thing you'd see would be the people.

(As TRACY *reads and* OLIVER *recites, we see* TODD, *in a hotel room in Times Square, unpacking a suitcase.)*

(In an Upper East Side mansion, HELEN *reads from a thick book and sips a glass of wine.)*

(In City Hall, DENISE POWELL *accompanies* JOHN KENDRICK *as he takes a seat in an armchair. He scans a sheet of paper and edits a word or two.)*

OLIVER: Like mites crawling across a map, one would be indistinguishable from the other.
Citizens appear, at first, not as individuals replete with minds and broken hearts and hopes and mortgages, but as a benign infestation. A single unit with a common goal: survival.

(TODD *stops unpacking and pulls out his cell phone. He sits, prepares to dial, then waits.*)

OLIVER: Yes, this is the only true way to enter New York City. From above.

The great dirigible should glide into place just above Three-fifty Fifth Avenue. The Empire State Building.	TRACY: *(Laughing)* Dirigible?

OLIVER: One ought to press his forehead against the glass panes and squint down at the street below.

(JOHN *hands* DENISE *the paper he was reading.*)

OLIVER: When the mooring rope is affixed to the edifice, one should take care with his hat, lest it fly away; a hat, after all, is imperative for the entrance.	DENISE: You're sure you're all— (JOHN *nods.*) Thirty seconds.

DENISE: Excuse me, for a moment, John… (*She walks out of the room into the hallway.*)

OLIVER: A gangplank must be extended, and one ought to savor that first step onto the one-hundred second floor.

(TODD *dials the phone.*)

(HELEN's *phone rings—a landline.*)

OLIVER: Breathe. Carve in granite the smell of a thousand feet high. Take the vintage Otis to the ground floor and disembark prepared for the spin through the revolving door and a whirling expulsion into the City.

(DENISE *breathes deeply, struggling to hold something back.*)

OLIVER: Remember the mites and the thin air and Fifth Avenue from above.	HELEN: *(Answering the phone)* Hello?

HELEN: Hello? Who is this?

A Prologue

OLIVER: Remember where you were before the blimp, before the sky.

(DENISE *gains control over herself. She straightens out her hair, her clothes.*)

OLIVER: Because when one steps out into the beating heart of New York City for the first time—having descended from the clouds—

TODD: Hi, it's— It's me.

OLIVER: —it's a resurrection.

(DENISE *walks back into the room with* JOHN.)

(OLIVER *pauses, an air of melancholy about him.*)

OLIVER: But no one makes that entrance anymore.

DENISE: John…

OLIVER: *(Looking right at* TRACY*)* Someday they will again.

DENISE: John, are you frightened?

TODD: Where are you?

OLIVER: Someday, it will be the only way.

DENISE: You're up.

OLIVER: From above.

(Beat)

TRACY: What?

ACT ONE

Scene One

(MAYOR JOHN KENDRICK *sits in a plush armchair, sipping from a glass of iced tea, addressing his constituents on live television. He's very thin, almost gaunt. His neatly pressed suit hangs off his frame.*)

JOHN: Good afternoon, my fellow New Yorkers. Hot as a brick oven, out there, isn't it? And they said Manhattan wasn't an island paradise. (*He chuckles.*) Nearly fifteen years ago, I stood on the steps of City Hall, from where I'm speaking to you now, and I asked you if I could be your heart. And I have been. For fourteen years, I've pumped tirelessly. Through prosperity into inevitable moments of dereliction and back again, I have led you fine New Yorkers. But more importantly, you have followed.

After the horrific events of the Thanksgiving Day Massacre, I asked you to trust in me. When homelessness and crime and poverty poured over the confines of a civilized society, I asked you to trust in me. When the work that my administration needed to accomplish outlasted the limitations of bureaucracy, I asked you to trust in me. And you did.

Tonight, on the brink of upheaval, I must ask again.

We have reached a great turning point in our city's history. A foe we thought had long since been vanquished has resurfaced. Only days ago, our administration received a missive from a citizen or group of citizens claiming to be representative of the Derelict threat. Once again, they plan on taking aim at this great building, this symbol of the administration that has kept them at bay for over a decade: City Hall. *(Pausing for a moment, he sips from the iced tea. He looks exhausted but rallies his energy. He stops reading his speech—the rest is off the cuff.)* This building, like all edifices in your great metropolis, was born of the blood and muscle of your fathers and of theirs. They did not succumb. Nor will we. I speak to you tonight from City Hall because this administration will not cowtow to fear.

My fellow New Yorkers. We can face the impending wave alone and in dread, or we can board the ship together and rise above the swell. But we must act, we must act before it pulls us under, extinguishing this city's life forever.

Once again, I am asking you to follow me.

Because, once again, that life is in danger.

Scene Two

(Late that afternoon. Seated on the bed of a moderately priced hotel room in Times Square, TODD *turns his cell phone over in his hands. He's wearing a tucked in button-up shirt and a tie. In this outfit, he is the definition of a square.* TRACY *bursts into the room, feverishly typing on her cell phone and chewing gum.)*

TRACY: Fear mongering! Did you see that? That speech? Good Mister Mayor's—
(Searching for the word:) On the, uh… —On the…

TODD: Television?

TRACY: Did you see it?

TODD: I didn't.

TRACY: Fear mongering!

TODD: You said. / Tracy, I was thinking, about tonight—

TRACY: They were playing it out on the, uh on those big screens in Times Square. Next to that giant photo of— It's terrifying. It is. What really frustrates— Okay, I mean, okay, they don't know Thing One about this threat and he's in front of a camera just to, like, what— to sew seeds of panic? As if they couldn't deal with this quietly, without all the sturm und drang.

TODD: Us? We don't live here.

TRACY: The inclusive "us." Like, humankind. Look, I know you haven't been home in years, but you still must feel *some* amount of ownership over this city. I mean, I do, and I haven't even visited since I was, like, three. Plus, Todd, Kendrick is part of the contemporary American political scene. It's my job to be informed about— Well, someday it would be nice if it were my job to be informed about these things. *(She's on her phone again, typing)* God, he's horrific. Where the Coca-Cola ad used to be, where they drop the ball every— Now there's just that enormous picture of Good Mister Mayor. Everyone in this city is just— Ugh, they're infatuated. He's like Manhattan's version of...you know, the, uh, the... Come on, you know who I'm talking about... That guy. I can't believe I'm blanking...

TODD: Maybe try detaching your thumbs from the phone for fifteen seconds. You're worse than my students. How do type that fast?

TRACY: *(Smiling)* Well, it's certainly gotten more difficult with this in the way. *(She wiggles her occupied ring finger and gets back to typing.)*

TODD: Good thing I didn't spring for the whole half-carat.

TRACY: *(Still typing)* Good thing. *(Suddenly:)* Mussolini! Manhattan's Mussolini!

TODD: Of course.

TRACY: Todd, this Good Mister Mayor stuff, it's fantastic. I mean, it's awful, but it's fucking fantastic! *(Typing furiously)* One sec...
What's another word for "power-grubbing fascist puppetmaster?"

TODD: I don't... Megalomaniac?

TRACY: Too many characters. *(She finishes typing as she talks.)* I'm starting to think— oh! Svengali! duh—I'm starting to think maybe this could actually put me on the map.

TODD: I thought live-tweeting the trip was just an exercise, a little sidebar to your Dispatch article about travelling in the Big Not-So-Bad City.

TRACY: I love you, kiddo, I do, but you've really got to get over this holier-than-thou, anti-progressive, condescensing, aversive terror of technology.

TODD: I'm not allowed to mourn the death of individualism? The end of privacy?

TRACY: No, Todd. You're not. These technologies aren't fads, they aren't fly-by-night, you know, experiments. They're not— This is as close as human beings have ever come to, to genuine, literal democracy.

TODD: *(Overlapping with below)* Oh come on. Come. On.

TRACY: *(Overlapping with above)* No, Todd, No. See? Condescensing.
Following, reposting, liking, what are those if not votes?

TODD: To what end? Sharing videos of adorable pistachios?

TRACY: God, you're so— What are adorable pistachios? Todd, this interconnectivity has toppled regimes, built nations, brought people together to change the world, make it a safer, more equitable place to live. Democracy's a powerful tool. One we all *(Waving her phone in his face)* must wield. Don't poo-poo.

TODD: All I'm saying, *Che*, is that I don't want access to anyone else's life, and I don't want anyone else having access to mine. Okay? That's it.

TRACY: Like your life is so interesting. Believe what you want, but Twitter's going to be my key to—I mean, if this Derelicts thing pans out / like I think it might then—

TODD: Did you say Derelicts—?

TRACY: Yeah. There's been a letter from the Derelicts. A threat. *(Channeling* Poltergeist II:*)* They're baaaack. Which may mean—fingers crossed—an accidental goldmine for me.

TODD: Wait, what about the Derelicts? What happened?

(TRACY presses "post" and really gives TODD a once over for the first time.)

TRACY: Well, don't you look…nifty.

TODD: You don't like the outfit?

TRACY: No. I think you're going to be the belle of the sockhop. Glad to see people still get dressed for the theater.

TODD: I thought it would be nice if I looked…

TRACY: Like a closeted Presbyterian youth minister?

TODD: Actually, Tracy, I think I'm gonna pass on the play tonight. I made, um, dinner...plans...

TRACY: Wait—*dinner*? Todd, dinner? Tonight? Tonight, Todd? Dinner? Tonight? With her?

(TODD doesn't answer.)

TRACY: Shit, give me a second. *(She rushes into the bathroom to change. From off:)* When did you decide this? *(She pops her head back into the room.)* Do I have time to shower? Fuck it. I'll run my head under the sink. *(She pops back out.)*

TODD: You know what? You go to the play. I don't want to make you come all the way to the East Side with me. The food at Ruby's isn't even very good. Meat's always overcooked...

TRACY: *(From off)* The food? You think I give even half a hoot about the— You're nuts, you know that?

TODD: Go. It's gotten good reviews.

TRACY: *(From off)* Who gives a shit about reviews? I'm coming to dinner.

TODD: No, Tracy, I don't want to make you go through this whole rigmarole.

TRACY: *(From off)* I can handle a rigamarole. *(She reenters in a robe with moist hair. She's spit out her gum.)* Under certain circumstances, I'm extremely charming.

TODD: Honestly, it's just not worth it.

TRACY: To meet the woman who pushed the man I'm spending the rest of my life with into the world? Yeah. It is.

TODD: You weren't planning on meeting her this trip anyway. I didn't even decide to call her until today.

TRACY: This is a joke, right? You're joking. This is your attempt at a joke.

TODD: Tracy…

TRACY: Noble effort, Todd. Nice try, really, but… you know you're not funny.

TODD: Yeah, you keep saying that…

TRACY: *(Unzipping her suitcase)* How nice is this restaurant? What did you say it was called? Ruby's?

TODD: Tracy, I'd rather you—I don't think it's a good idea is all I'm saying.

TRACY: You came here with me so you could show me where you come from. Don't you think Mom might be a teeny-tiny part of that?
Todd, I've been begging you to take me to the City for years and finally, *finally*… We're here. She's here…

TODD: I'm sorry, Tracy, but I think it's… Yeah, it's case closed.

TRACY: Not closed. This is still open. Case open!

TODD: Tracy. Enough, okay? I'm late.

TRACY: Oh, I see. You're embarrassed of me.

TODD: Why would you possibly say / something like that?

TRACY: It's the only thing I can think of. You're embarrassed of me wagging my lefty liberal quarter-carat adorned finger in your conservative mama's face. / Which I will not do. I will behave.

TODD: Why would I ever be embarrassed / of you?

TRACY: Because that's / the only excuse I can think of for you—

TODD: If anything it's you / who should be, you know, of me.

TRACY: Yeah, well no one said I wasn't. Would you keep your voice down?

TODD: Oh, *I* should keep my voice down?

TRACY: Todd, why can't I come?

TODD: I want her to take some time to get used to the idea of you.

TRACY: She'll love me. What's not to like about me?

(TODD *sits next to* TRACY *on the bed.*)

TODD: Nothing. Nothing. You're perfect.

TRACY: Not perfect. I'm in love with *you.*

TODD: There's a reason my mother and I haven't spoken in this long. Tracy, it's got nothing to do with you and me.

TRACY: Is this about your dad's, um, the inheritance?

TODD: Yeah, honestly. It is.

TRACY: You haven't seen her since the funeral?

TODD: Since… Yeah, no.

TRACY: I think he would have liked me. Your dad. The great Jacob Nevelson. What did he do again? Insurance?

TODD: Life.

TRACY: Life insurance. Yeah, he definitely would have liked me. I have a way with actuaries.

TODD: Tracy, I am seeing my mother tonight so I can tell her that I'm engaged to a very intelligent, very stubborn, very beautiful but very stubborn girl. But—

TRACY: Todd—

TODD: *But* it would mean a lot to me if you let me do this alone. Things with my mother are… It's complicated. Will you let me do that, Tracy? Please?

TRACY: Todd… No.

(TODD *kisses* TRACY. *He stands to leave.*)

TRACY: Don't order wine. You know you can't handle wine.

TODD: I'll call you when I'm done.

TRACY: You are one hell of an enigma, Todd Nevelson, you know that?

TODD: Let me know how you like the play.

(TODD *exits.* TRACY *slumps onto the bed, dejected. Her phone dings.*)

Scene Three

(*The same evening, sunset.* OLIVER *stands at a railing in Battery Park, staring out over the water. He has a briefcase at his side and is holding an already-opened envelope.* DENISE *approaches in a rush.*)

DENISE: Ten minutes.

OLIVER: (*Staring out at the harbor*) Do you ever think she gets lonely out there alone on that rock?

DENISE: That's a hard ten minutes, Oliver.

OLIVER: That torch looks heavy; she must be exhausted. (*Little beat*) You think she misses France?

DENISE: Can whatever this is wait? In case you haven't noticed, today's been... (*Small beat*) Okay, what? What's the matter?

(OLIVER *holds up the envelope.*)

DENISE: Oh, Oliver, I'm sorry. Another one? Who was it this time?

OLIVER: Grove Atlantic.

DENISE: (*Trying to cheer him up, a joke they've told before*) Grove Atlantic? Charlatans!

OLIVER: (*Only half playing along*) Philistines!

DENISE: What did they say? (*He hands her the envelope.*) "Florid, verbose…" "Patently unpublishable…" Oof. "While your view of New York City's history as an ongoing spiral toward self-destruction terrifies, your theories remain an unfounded fiction."
What does that mean?

OLIVER: I don't know why they don't see. It's obvious. For five-hundred years we've been headed toward this moment. The city's a rubber band, pulled tight by fear, ready to snap.

DENISE: You do understand why not everyone sees it that way, yes? Your wife, for instance.

OLIVER: I'm not criticizing your work or Kendrick's administration or—

DENISE: I know.

OLIVER: It's merely inevitable. A government powered by fear's the most efficient, hence the most likely eventual outcome. People here are terrified. Always angry and afraid, with no outlet. The dam's about to burst. The least I can do is try to explain how we got here.

DENISE: Oliver, maybe no one wants to hear this because they like feeling safe. They are safe.

OLIVER: Safe and afraid aren't mutually exclusive. I'm exhausted, Denise. This is exhausting.

DENISE: I know, Oliver. I know.

OLIVER: The burden of being ignored's a heavy one. My heart's with Cassandra.

(*Small beat.* DENISE *is anxious to move this along.*)

DENISE: So where was it this time?

OLIVER: The Empire State Building.

DENISE: You go all the way to the top?

OLIVER: To the observation deck. This time, Denise, this time I was really going to do it. Call it quits. I went to the edge and I looked out and took the first pages out of my briefcase—I'd been rewriting the Prologue this morning, which I guess is maybe why I decided to go up the— I don't know. I took the first page, and I held it out over the metal railing and I just... *(He mimes dropping a page over the railing.)* Then I tossed another. And another. I watched to see how far they'd float. Where they'd reach. A single sheet from a hundred stories gets a life of its own on the way down, like a gull's ghost haunting the skies.

DENISE: *(Surreptitiously checking her watch)* How far did they get?

OLIVER: I have no idea. A guard grabbed me, told me it was littering. I tried elucidating the futility of the creative process and, well, some people just don't appreciate the subtleties of a metaphorical unburdening. Chalk up one more in a day's torrent of failure.
But when the guard tossed me out onto Fifth Avenue, I saw someone. A woman. She was smoking a cigarette and she was reading one of the pages that had fallen. And the thing is, she smiled. She liked it. I could tell. She was reading *The Chronicle of the City of New York* and she liked it!

DENISE: But it was the only the first page, right? The book is—how long is it now?

OLIVER: Five.

DENISE: Yeah. Five-thousand pages.

OLIVER: Well, four-thousand / eight-hundred sixteen.

DENISE: Oliver.

OLIVER: It's comprehensive.

DENISE: In this case, I'd say comprehensive is a euphemism.

OLIVER: You think I should, what, just give up?

DENISE: Oliver, I'm proud of you. You set out to achieve something, and you did. So what if the publishers don't understand it. Fuck the publishers. They're a bunch of tripe-pushing failed novelists and literary groupies with a requisite taste for the rectum.

OLIVER: You think I should give up?

DENISE: You're the one who said you were thinking about/ quitting, I was only—

OLIVER: If I do, then what have I been doing for the last ten years?

DENISE: When we decided you would quit the law firm to write this, what did we say? We said there's nothing worse than wondering "what if."

OLIVER: *Knowing* what if's not much better.

DENISE: And, yeah, we also said that if it didn't work out, if the book didn't come together as you'd hoped…

OLIVER: But she liked it! The woman with the cigarette, she liked it!

DENISE: That's one person. How many publishers have told you "no"?

OLIVER: What happened to "fuck 'em"?

DENISE: Maybe you should take a break. Take some time off. One person liking one page doesn't mean—

OLIVER: History has turned on one person.

DENISE: Yeah, maybe, Oliver, that might be true. But to have your work published, you need a lot more than one. So, okay. Maybe an epic, unfinished history of the eventual, inevitable destruction of New York City recounted in prose-poem doesn't have the audience we'd hoped.

OLIVER: *The Chronicle* lacks details. That's its shortfall.

DENISE: It's five-thousand pages long.

OLIVER: They say it's a fiction, that I'm seeing something that's not there.

DENISE: Oliver, it might be time to —

OLIVER: I need your help.

DENISE: If you want me to read it, maybe once everything's slowed down with this new threat…

OLIVER: No.

DENISE: I know. Not till it's finished.

OLIVER: No, what I need is proof, proof that this administration is headed down this path.

DENISE: Oliver.

OLIVER: I know the city maintains records of all internal memos, meeting minutes, emails stretching back decades. If I could find something no one's found before…

DENISE: You're grasping at straws.

OLIVER: I'm not, Denise. I'm not, I…I know what I'm after. What's the one part of this city's history more shrouded in secrecy than any other? There has to be a record, there has to be of what happened within this city's government twelve years ago in the months and years following the Thanksgiving Day Massacre.

DENISE: And you think you're the guy to publish that record?

OLIVER: None of this would implicate you—it's all before you were in City Hall.

DENISE: It's not me I'm concerned about.

OLIVER: Him?

(Small beat)

DENISE: What do you expect to find in City Hall that the whole world doesn't know already?

OLIVER: I don't know.

DENISE: *(Concurrent with below)* See, this is—

OLIVER: *(Concurrent with above)* But something no one's seen.

DENISE: Because those documents are classified, Oliver. No one's seen it because it's classified. By executive order. Every bit of information regarding the Derelicts is classified.

OLIVER: Which is why I have an advantage no other author's got.

DENISE: What's that?

OLIVER: You. You have access.

DENISE: Yes, I do.

OLIVER: So take me.

DENISE: I could be arrested. As could you.

OLIVER: Why are they under lock and key? Isn't transparency our constitutional right?

DENISE: It's not, Oliver. The government's role is to protect its citizens. We tried transparency and look what happened. The Derelicts had access to information that allowed them to bomb Gracie Mansion, to target government officials. They would have taken out City Hall if they hadn't— Did you not see the news today? Did you not see John on television?

OLIVER: Which only proves my—

DENISE: Now of all times, Oliver, do you really want to be caught rifling through classified documents? For what? For some half-baked history book? *(Small beat)* That's not what I— Jesus, Oliver. / It's been a long day. I'm—

OLIVER: *(Concurrent with above)* This isn't just a book *about* history. It *is* history. It's time itself. Definitive. Absolute.
The Chronicle's not complete. When it's finished, it'll sell.

DENISE: Is this about money? We're fine. / We don't need—

OLIVER: What good's having the truth if no one sees it. No, this is about getting my words out into the world. Seeing my book on a shelf.

DENISE: Pretty big shelf...

OLIVER: Denise—

DENISE: Oliver, please don't ask me for this.

OLIVER: Then let me go. You don't have to come. If I get caught, I'll take the blame. Give me your access I D and I'll go alone.

DENISE: They'll be able to trace it back to me, Oliver. It's all digital.

OLIVER: So what do you want me to do?

DENISE: Take a break, like I said. Maybe go back to the firm for a bit.

OLIVER: You know how miserable I was there.

DENISE: How miserable are you now? You've been working on this for years. At some point, you've got to let reality in.
We'll talk about this later. I'm sorry, Oliver, I have to go.

OLIVER: He can wait. I'm in crisis.

DENISE: Crisis? My office, this *city* is the target of a threat. That is a crisis. This…this is melodrama. I don't have the energy for this right now.

OLIVER: I don't understand. You're not a doctor. No one's life is at stake.

DENISE: Eight million lives are at stake, Oliver. Eight million. Every fucking day.

Scene Four

(TODD *and* HELEN *sit across from each other in the dining room of Ruby's, an elegant Upper East Side Italian restaurant. As he speaks, she looks around the room, only half paying attention.*)

TODD: It's a tough age, middle school. And, of course, I know pre-algebra's not going to be their priority. But holding their attention's only getting more and more difficult. Even as I get better and my style gets more, you know, refined—and I have a good lesson plan, I'm proud of it—it amazes me how every year, I feel my presence as a live, human person in the room interests them less and less.

HELEN: You were a nightmare in junior high. Headstrong, stubborn.

TODD: The good news is other than grading tests, homework, I can leave my work at work. I love it, I do, you know, but it's not my life.

HELEN: In those days, you were so much worse to me than you were to your father.

TODD: Jesus. Already? Wonderful.

HELEN: Did I say something wrong?

TODD: I knew this would happen. I fucking knew it.

HELEN: Profanity, Toddie. It's the idiot's wheelhouse.

TODD: This is why. This, right here.

HELEN: I'm sorry, did I say something to upset you?

TODD: I told you I didn't want to talk about it, so why do you push?

HELEN: I thought we were talking about your geometry class.

TODD: Don't play dumb.

HELEN: If you don't want to talk about it, why are you here?

TODD: Because you begged me to come. You called me and you told me you needed my help.

HELEN: I wasn't aware that berating your mother qualified as "help."

TODD: What do you want from me?

HELEN: I told you. I want you to stay.

TODD: And I told you, three days and we're gone.

HELEN: We?

TODD: Yeah, you and me. We're done. You have me for three days. So what do you want, Mother?

HELEN: *(Picking up the menu)* What looks good to you?

TODD: That's not what I— Ugh, you're impossible. *(Sighs)* I don't know. The skate maybe.

HELEN: You hate fish.

TODD: Yeah, I used to.

(Small beat)

HELEN: Do you have any questions? Anything you'd like to ask?

TODD: What did I *just* say?

(Beat)

HELEN: So, what's next? After middle school math?

TODD: I don't know. Retirement?

HELEN: A life cramming times tables into the thick heads of the progeny of Middle America.

TODD: Take a napkin. You've got some disdain dripping down your chin.

HELEN: You're wasting your talents.

TODD: I'm using them. Teaching is a noble profession.

HELEN: So's garbage collection.

TODD: Where is the waiter?

HELEN: Okay, Toddie. Okay. I get it. You don't want to make waves. You've settled for a life of still waters. But eight years? You've made your point. Enough's enough. You've wandered the desert. Come home.

TODD: *(Frantically looking around the room)* Even a busboy maybe…

HELEN: Toddie, I need you to stay in New York. Just for the summer. Then you can go.

TODD: You know I can't.

HELEN: What have you got keeping you there? A lease on a one-bedroom condo?

TODD: I shouldn't have… This was a mistake.

HELEN: For me, Toddie. Not for him.

TODD: *(Craning his neck around the room)* Does no one work at this restaurant? *(He sees something. His face loses all its color.)* Oh, you've got to be fucking kidding.

HELEN: Idiot's wheelhouse.

TODD: Jesus.

HELEN: What? What's the matter?

(TRACY *enters looking confused. She's on her phone, scanning the restaurant.*)

TRACY: *(On the phone)* Hi, sweetie. It's Tracy. Just calling to, uh, check in to see how things are going with Mom. That's all, just...

TODD: *(To* HELEN*)* Would you excuse me for a second?

(TODD *gets up and goes over to* TRACY.)

TRACY: *(Still on the phone, her back to* TODD*)* It's intermission and the play is really...fascinating. Lots of...words...and...acting ...

(TRACY *turns to see* TODD *right alongside her. Still into the phone:)*

TRACY: Well, I'm looking right at you now. You look... not happy. But handsome. So, when you're listening to this message remember how much I love you and how embarrassed you were for yelling at me in a crowded restaurant. Okay bye. *(She hangs up.)* Hi! This place is fancy.

TODD: You're supposed to be at the play.

TRACY: Oh, kiddo, you know me better than that.

TODD: Tracy, you have to leave.

TRACY: I'm already here. The worst part is over.

TODD: Please, Tracy— Please just take a cab back to the hotel—

TRACY: *(Catching sight of* HELEN*)* Oh my god, is that her? *(She waves at* HELEN.*)* That's her. I love her. I'm gonna to say hi.

TODD: Don't you dare say hi.

TRACY: *(To* HELEN, *from across the room)* Hi! *(To* TODD:*)* Oops.

(TRACY *walks over to* HELEN.)

TRACY: Hi. I can't tell you how thrilled I am to meet you.

HELEN: All right.

(Long beat)

TRACY: And I must be Tracy.

TODD: She was just leaving.

HELEN: Were you? That's a shame. Where are you headed?

TRACY: *(Extremely nervous)* Todd here wants me to go back to the hotel. Honestly, he didn't even want me to come tonight. We had tickets to see some play off-Broadway. But I sold them to a very nice Japanese couple in the lobby. Well, they might have been Korean, I don't know. It's hard to tell—I mean, I didn't ask.

TODD: Tracy—

TRACY: *(To* HELEN*)* God, you're so beautiful. I can see where Todd gets his— And elegant! Todd, never mentioned how elegant you were. You look like a—I don't know—like a nineteenth century Russian Tzarina or something. Like a Romanoff. Like a sexy Romanoff.

TODD: Oh my god.

TRACY: I love that dress. Is that cotton? Synthetic. Do you mind if I touch— I'm not gonna touch it. It's your dress. Why would I— What?
I can't believe I'm finally meeting you...Mom. *(To* TODD*)* That was too soon. I can see that.

TODD: Tracy!

HELEN: And how do you know Toddie?

TRACY: Didn't he tell you we— Wait. *Toddie?*

TODD: Jesus.

TRACY: Did she just call you "Toddie?"

HELEN: What did he—?

TRACY: Toddie! Oh, that is certainly something to keep in my back pocket.

TODD: Mother, this is Tracy Holstein. She's my, uh…

TRACY: Fiancée. *(To* HELEN:*)* Has he always been this awkward or is this, like, a recent development?

HELEN: I see. Well, then, congratulations.

TRACY: *(To* TODD*)* You didn't tell her? *(To* HELEN:*)* He didn't tell you? Did he even mention me?

HELEN: I can't imagine how I could forget hearing about *you.*

TRACY: That son of a bitch. *(To* HELEN:*)* No offense. You're not a…

TODD: Oh my god.

TRACY: I'm mortified.

HELEN: Don't be. My son's not what I'd call an open book. You should have told me when I called, Toddie. I would have given you Gram's ring.

TRACY: *(To* TODD*) She* called *you?* I thought— *(To* HELEN:*)* I'm sorry what ring?

HELEN: His grandmother's diamond. It's a family heirloom. But yours seems lovely. What is that, a half-carat?

TODD: Almost.

TRACY: It's plenty. *(To* TODD:*)* But if it would mean more to you if I wore a family heirloom, I could always—

TODD: Mother, Tracy was just leaving.

TRACY: Was I?

TODD: I'm not going to ask you again, okay?

HELEN: It was lovely to meet you, Miss Holstein.

TRACY: I could stay for a little while—

TODD: Now I'm begging, Tracy. Leave.

TRACY: I'm already here. Why don't I just sit down, stay for dinner. I won't say a word. I'll be as quiet as a— *(Looking out the widow:)* Holy shit! Holy shit, Todd.

TODD: What?

TRACY: Oh my god oh my god oh my god. Yes.

TODD: *(To* HELEN, *with disbelief)* You didn't—

*(*HELEN *shrugs.)*

TODD: *(Concurrent with below)* You're unbelievable, you know that? You promised me you wouldn't ambush me like this.

TRACY: *(Concurrent with above)* Todd. Todd. He's coming in here. Here. This is insane. Of all places in the whole city! This is absolutely insane!

HELEN: Miss Holstein, I couldn't have put it better myself.

TODD: Jesus.

*(*HELEN *shrugs.* JOHN *walks into the restaurant and approaches their table.)*

JOHN: Sorry I'm late. As you can imagine, today's been a whopper. Good to see you, Toddie.

*(*TODD *doesn't respond.)*

JOHN: And who is this lovely young woman?

HELEN: John, I'd like you to meet Tracy Holstein. Your future daughter-in-law.

(Beat)

TRACY: Holy fucking shit.

Scene Five

(That night. OLIVER *sits on the stoop of his West
Village brownstone, a metal trashcan at his feet.* DENISE
approaches.)

DENISE: Do you mind?

*(*OLIVER *shrugs.* DENISE *sits next to him on the stoop. She
looks up at the sky.)*

DENISE: Not a single star. That's my least favorite thing
about the city. You can never see the stars. It's like
living—

OLIVER: In a basement. You've said.

DENISE: I'm surprised to see you out here.

OLIVER: On our stoop?

DENISE: You haven't smoked in, what, ten years?

OLIVER: I'm not smoking. *(He holds up a large stack of
papers and gestures to a full banker's box alongside him
on the stoop.)* I'm cremating. *(He looks at the pages.)* The
whole *Chronicle.* All going the way of Joan of Arc.

DENISE: Oh.
You sure?

OLIVER: I'm done. Like you said, eventually you have
to let reality in. What's the point of shouting if no one's
going to listen. Maybe Cassandra should have cut her
losses.

DENISE: Oliver. I'm proud of you.

OLIVER: So some of *The Chronicle* will be lost to the
wind. The rest to the flame. An unfinished… *(Beat)*
Here goes.

*(*OLIVER *tosses the stack into the trash can. He pulls out
a box of matches. He hesitates for a moment, nervous. He
lights a match and tosses it into the trashcan. It bursts into*

flames. DENISE *sits behind him and kisses his neck. She rubs his shoulders.)*

DENISE: I like this. It's like a, like a Viking funeral.

(OLIVER *chuckles.)*

DENISE: It's all right, you know. Everything comes to an end.

OLIVER: Everything?

(OLIVER *turns around and kisses* DENISE. *She pulls back, smiles. He stares at her.)*

DENISE: What?

OLIVER: You're a vision, Denise, you know that?

DENISE: I'm exhausted.

OLIVER: You look exactly like how I imagine Cleopatra. My queen of the Hudson.

DENISE: Come inside, Oliver.

OLIVER: I think...I think I need to stay. For a minute.

(Small beat)

DENISE: You know, the timing of this is— Today, after I got back to the office, I called the firm.

OLIVER: Why?

DENISE: I set up a meeting for next week. They said they'd love to have you back.

OLIVER: Oh.

DENISE: They want you back! It's fantastic! Isn't that fantastic?
You don't think that's fantastic.

OLIVER: You didn't know I was letting *The Chronicle* go until tonight.

DENISE: Yeah, but, Oliver, how many times have you gone to the Empire State Building or the Statue of

Liberty or the Chrysler Building or the Brooklyn Bridge
or the Central Park Reservoir to dump this thing? *"I'm
finished. I'm done. No more."* And then you come
back, you plug in your flash drive, print out another
copy and keep writing. We spend less on food than we
do on toner.
I can see how much pain this work is causing you.
You're afraid that if you stop it'll feel like you quit, like
you failed. I get that. But you didn't. You could never,
as far as I'm concerned. Calling the firm, I'm just trying
to maybe help you take that step forward.

OLIVER: Forward? To the job that's already sucked up
eleven years of my life?

DENISE: It's a good firm. You like those guys.

(Small beat)

OLIVER: When I was in grade school, I used to go into
the library in Bryant Park and head straight for the
card catalog. I'd pick a letter and I'd slide out that
narrow drawer and I'd read the cards. Just last name,
first name, title. Last name, first name, title. Last name,
first name…
There's no vocation nobler than the burden borne by
him who keeps the record.

DENISE: Huh. That's…huh. Who said that?

(OLIVER gestures, indicating himself.)

DENISE: Course.

OLIVER: When I was working on *The Chronicle*, Denise, I
could feel the pull of this direct line from Heroditus to
me. And from me *(Makes a "whoosh" sound and follows
his hand out toward the horizon)* right into the future.
Thousands of years on either end collapsing from both
directions into one point: Oliver Judd.

DENISE: But Oliver, I think you've got to listen to what the world wants from you. Maybe Grove Atlantic passing this last time, maybe that's the world trying to tell you something.

OLIVER: Maybe it's you trying to tell me something. *(Beat)* I asked you for one thing. All you had to do was let me see the records in the basement of City Hall...

DENISE: Please, Oliver, can we put this behind us?

OLIVER: I could have found something in there—

DENISE: *(Concurrent with below)* There's nothing to find.

OLIVER: *(Concurrent with above)* — and I could have finished *The Chronicle*. Ten years...for this? *(He kicks the trash can.)*

DENISE: Don't go back to the firm, Oliver, if it won't make you happy. Any number of firms would love to have you. Or don't work in law at all, I don't care. You could teach! Or go back to school. Or... *(Beat)* I'm sorry I...couldn't give you what you needed. You do understand, yeah? You forgive me?

(After a moment, OLIVER nods.)

DENISE: Good, because— That's...that's good. *(She kisses him.)* Oliver...because things are about to change. For both of us. And I'm gonna need your help.

Scene Six

(Back at Ruby's, after dinner. By now, TRACY, TODD, JOHN and HELEN are all sitting around the table. TODD nurses a large glass of wine, which he is periodically refilling. Throughout, JOHN drinks repeatedly from a glass of water, never touching the wine.)

TRACY: Because for twelve years, you've been exploiting the events of the Thanksgiving Day

Massacre to maintain—I don't know—Svengali-like power over a city of under-informed, overly suspicious individuals!

JOHN: Svenagli?

TODD: Like an evil hypnotist.

JOHN: *(Concurrent with below)* I know what a Svengali—

HELEN: *(Concurrent with above)* He knows.

TRACY: I mean, why make the public aware of this latest threat to begin with? The only explanation I can think of is that, like always, you're trying to spread fear far and wide, keep the entire city enrolled as card-carrying members of the Cult of Kendrick.

JOHN: It's interesting you should mention a cult, Ms Holstein, since it's precisely the cult of the Derelicts from which my administration has been protecting this city for the past twelve years.

TRACY: A cult! These people were a disparate group of homeless men and women before they, you know, galvanized and revolted. And—

TODD: Tracy…

TRACY: And they wouldn't have even been homeless in the first place if your administration hadn't forced them onto the streets.

JOHN: Forced them?

HELEN: Are you defending this sort of violence?

TRACY: Of course not! Violence is— I mean, of course it's never the answer. Never. Okay, except for, like, World War Two, but that's— I mean.

JOHN: *(To TODD)* When did you say the wedding was going to be?

TRACY: But regardless, it's misleading and and and wrongheaded to refer to them as a cult.

HELEN: They were— They are an Anarchist cult.

TRACY: Hold up, Mrs K. Are they anarchists or are they a cult?

HELEN: They targeted Macy's, City Hall and Gracie Mansion: centers of commerce, leadership and government. That's anarchism.

TRACY: No! Why don't you— They were fighting for their rights!

HELEN: What you're referring to aren't rights. They're entitlements.

TRACY: Are you kidding me? Are you kidding me?

JOHN: Ms Holstein—

HELEN: It sounds an awful lot to me as though you're taking a viewpoint quite divorced from reality. You're excusing their violence.

(JOHN *leans back and takes a deep breath.* HELEN *hands him a glass of water.*)

HELEN: *(To* JOHN*)* Here.

(JOHN *waves it away.*)

JOHN: Toddie, what're you thinking of the Cardinals' lineup this year? Think they've got a chance against our boys in blue and orange?

TRACY: You're a Mets fan? Talk about divorced from reality—
Okay, what I'm saying—what am I saying? —I'm saying we need to back up.

TODD: How bout we go back up to the hotel? / Get it? Okay, let's go.

TRACY: I'm saying that the course of events is clear. When your administration, Mayor Kendrick—

JOHN: Call me John.

TODD: *(Under his breath)* Jesus Christ.

JOHN: *(To* TODD, *concurrent with below)* Did I say something wrong?

TRACY: *(Concurrent with above)* When you cut funding to publicly run shelters, subsidized housing, social services for the underprivileged, you created a homeless population larger than any in this city's history, which / went on to—

JOHN: Those cuts you mention were enacted by my predecessor. And they'd been proposed by the three mayoral administrations before my mine. That's how uncontroversial they were.

*(*JOHN *scratches his chest. When he hits his rib, he winces and clutches his side. He breathes deep and sips from his glass.)*

TRACY: One of those administrations being your father's! Mayor Kendrick, the first! Some dads pass down tire shops. You inherited a municipality. And good boy that you are, you accomplished what he couldn't because because you had the people in your pocket with all that fear bullshit.

HELEN: There's no need to resort to profanity, Ms Holstein.

TODD: *(Getting drunk)* Yeah, it's the idiot's wheelbarrow.

HELEN: This situation has got nothing to do with John's father. John inherited the conditions of this city from the previous administration. He didn't create the mess, he's cleaned it up.

TODD: Everybody's staring.

TRACY: Okay, let's ignore, for a minute, how the homeless population got there in the first place— *(Coughs and points her thumb at* JOHN:*)* ahem ahem —

HELEN: *(Concurrent with below)* Oh for the love of—

TRACY: *(Concurrent with above)* —once this massive number of people were tossed onto the street, they revolted, they galvanized. And they had every right to dissent!

JOHN: Our political process has acceptable, peaceful outlets for dissent—

TRACY: *(Concurrent with below)* Not anymore!

JOHN: *(Concurrent with above, worked up)* —but their "demand," as you have so glibbly labeled it, led to a series of protests, then riots, then, eventually the Thanksgiving Day attacks. Once violence enters the picture, circumstances become pretty darn hard to defend.

HELEN: I think that's enough.

(JOHN gestures: "It's okay" and leans back in his chair.)

JOHN: These people were insane. We took precautions.

TRACY: You have to look at where they're coming from.

HELEN: One forfeits one's right to sympathy when one turns to violence.

TRACY: Sympathy, maybe. But whether one is insane or one is not, the constitution of the United States—

TODD: *(Concurrent with below)* You're not going to win this, Tracy, you should—

TRACY: *(Concurrent with above)* —protects the rights of all its citizens, even those who choose violence. Even those you deem insane. Instead, what did they get? They got an executive order—without City Council approval or a public referendum—an order from you authorizing the N Y P D to establish a new arm of their military force specifically designated —

HELEN: *(Concurrent with below)* Military! Do you hear what you're saying?

TRACY: *(Concurrent with above)* —specifically designed to track down and eliminate the entirety of the homeless population. Then, you put the homeless, one by one, in front of classified panels to determine if they were part of the uprising.

JOHN: And if they were not, Ms Holstein—and most of them weren't—we placed them in publicly subsidized shelters and provided them resources to get them on their feet. Resulting, I may remind you, in the lowest number of homeless individuals per capita in the recorded history of this great city.
We'd identify the homeless and we'd help them. And the drop in homelessness has led to a drastic reduction in crime, drugs, violence.

HELEN: The city's safer than it's ever been.

TODD: *(Leaning over and taking his mother's glass)* You gonna finish that?

JOHN: As for the panels, yes, much of that is classified—

TRACY: *(Concurrent with below)* Obviously.

JOHN: *(Concurrent with above)* —but what I can tell you is that now we are prepared for their return. Which, I remind you, has occurred. We are prepared for what we as a city must face.

TRACY: So, all this fear mongering has nothing to do with your trying to dupe the public into repeatedly extending your term limits?

JOHN: That was a choice made by the people, by a vote, and with the approval of the City Council. *(He winces, breathes through it.)*

HELEN: Sometimes, Ms Holstein, a steady hand in the midst of the crisis is vital.

TRACY: Says Caesar.

HELEN: *(To* JOHN*)* It's like talking to a child.

JOHN: You're accusing me of subverting democracy for personal gains. Is that what you're saying?

TRACY: *(Building in intensity throughout)* I'm accusing you of using fear to manipulate the populace into relinquishing their democratic power, yes. You know what really built this country? The single act of an obscure Virginia farmer you may or may not have heard of.

George Washington.

You familiar? After his second term, he relinquished power. That one moment serves as the foundation for every principle our nation's built on today. It's the foundation of, say it with me now: Democracy. And look at you. You're on your fourth term, John! Jesus.

JOHN: But doesn't Democracy change? What it means to us can change. In Ancient Greece, democracy meant male born citizens voting by consensus. Literally, "rule by the people."

HELEN: Rule of the people, dear heart.

TRACY: But, of course, in our society, that's impractical. Still, it's a representative democracy.

JOHN: Our system has changed because our society has changed. If you explained today's version of democracy to the ancient Greeks, don't you think that the notion of electing representatives to make decisions on behalf of their constituents might seem like an unlawful ceding of power?

TRACY: Maybe, but—

JOHN: Society evolves, and so Democracy must evolve. As long as equality, which is at the heart of all notions of Democracy, as long as equality remains, power can be consolidated without a threat to the basis of a Democratic society.

TODD: *(Concurrent with below)* Could you all just stop this, please.

TRACY: *(Concurrent with above)* John, that is appalling.

HELEN: *(To* JOHN*)* It's fine, dear heart. Let it go.

JOHN: Progress leads us toward a singular vision: equality. So wouldn't the people bringing their voices together as one to change the current law and re-elect a representative dedicated to promoting a singular vision of safety and equality, wouldn't that in fact not be anti-democratic, not dictatorial, not totalitarian, but rather the logical evolution of American democracy at it's utmost?

TODD: My head is killing me.

TRACY: A singular vision is the exact opposite of Democracy! What you're describing is Nazi Germany /

(At the mention of the Nazis, HELEN, TODD *and* JOHN *all explode, speaking over one another:)*

TRACY: or Stalinism— Who said that all a leader requires to get the people on his side it to tell them they are being attacked and that pacifism is unpatriotic? Oh right, it was Goering! What you're saying is that as long as people feel that they're safe, the government should have free reign to—

HELEN: *(Concurrent with above and below)* When you bring Nazism into a discussion, you eliminate all room for debate. It's a misplayed trump card, Ms Holstein, and it hardly begins to apply to this situation. You can't bring up Nuremberg unless you plan on diving headfirst into that—

TODD: *(Concurrent with above and below)* Be quiet, please. Just stop this. Just—

JOHN: *(Concurrent with above)* You're far from the only detractor I've spoken with, Ms Holstein, and your opinions are thoughtful and valid, but ultimately, you're underestimating the possibility of threat, which, just today, has become a—

TODD: *(Suddenly standing)* SHUT UP! FOR THE LOVE OF GOD SHUT. THE HELL. UP! All of you! Look around you. Look! *(To the rest of the restaurant:)* Okay, you can go back to your meals now! Eat. Put away all those, you know, those video cell phones, and mind your own business, and just eat your damn pasta! *(To his table:)* I've been sitting here for two hours listening to you all talk yourselves in circles and I can't listen to one more fucking word! All this… squacking! "Come to New York, Todd." "Introduce me to your mother, Todd." "You don't like fish, Todd." I do like fish, Mother!

You can talk yourselves around and around and around and around but why are none of you talking about the one thing you're all thinking? *(Shouting at another table:)* I said, eat your goddamn pasta!

HELEN: That's enough, Toddie…

TODD: Todd. Period. End of…name. Just Todd.

TRACY: Would you sit down?

JOHN: Toddie, you're drunk.

TODD: You're dying!

Look at you. You're not okay. You're not— You're disappearing— And you ask me about the Cardinals? You talk about—about policy? How are you all sitting here, winding yourselves up like this, rehashing the same arguments you've been having for a decade and a half? For whose benefit? You know what kind of man you are. *(To HELEN:)* You know what he's done.

TRACY: Todd. Sit down.

TODD: You can't brush cancer under the carpet. You can't pretend it's not there. *(He points at* JOHN:*)* It's there. A man's life is about to end. Forever. I've got to… *(He walks away from the table. He comes back, grabs a half-full bottle of wine and storms out.)*

(Beat)

JOHN: Who wants dessert?

Scene Seven

(Continued from Scene Five. OLIVER *and* DENISE, *still on the stoop.)*

DENISE: Stage-four Non-Hodgkin's lymphoma.

OLIVER: When were you going to tell me?

DENISE: I just found out myself. John told me today, right before he went on T V.

OLIVER: And he's not going to…

DENISE: He says he has two, three months on the outside.

OLIVER: How's he handling this?

(DENISE shrugs.)

OLIVER: How're you handling this?

(DENISE shakes her head.)

OLIVER: And then, when he's, uh, he's gone, what happens to you? You're just going to, what? Take over?

DENISE: As the First Deputy Mayor, if he's incapacitated, his responsibilities fall on me.

OLIVER: That's… This is a lot for one night.

DENISE: I know, Oliver. But we've known for a while this would be in the cards. It's what I've been working toward.

OLIVER: But three months…

(Beat. OLIVER *stares at* DENISE.*)*

DENISE: Would you stop staring at me like that? Oliver, what?

OLIVER: Back when we first started dating—do you remember this?—one night, after we'd seen some atrocious band playing some atrocious club in some atrocious neighborhood downtown, well, you'd been mainlining tequila, so I was walking you home. You were wearing those tights you always used to— Dear god, those tights. I almost flunked the bar because of those tights—No, you don't remember this? Well, we stopped for a falafel and the guy behind the counter refused to take your order because you were drunk and loud and incredibly beligerent, and so you leaned toward him, and for a second, it looked like you were gonna kiss him, and I remember thinking, "Uh oh. My mother was right about this girl." But instead you grabbed him by his shirt, and you got up on your toes, and you were leaning so your whole body was pressed against the counter, and you said to this poor guy, right in his face, you said, "One day, asshole, I am going to be the mayor of New York City. But for tonight, all I am is hungry. So give the mayor her fucking falafel."

DENISE: Don't ever tell that story to anyone.

OLIVER: "I am going to be the mayor of New York City." I thought you were joking. So I married you.

DENISE: Not all politicians are inherently evil.

OLIVER: I don't see how any human could posess the ego it takes to lead. Let alone…you. I always thought, I don't know, you'd grow out of it.

DENISE: I can affect change. Positive change. Isn't it my responsibility to try?

OLIVER: It won't be easy. People worship John. The Great Protector.

DENISE: We've got to be careful how we reveal the information about his illness, build a strategy. Which is...scary but it's exciting, you know? All that's going to be part of my job. Gaining their trust.

OLIVER: Which is a lot more difficult when you're husband's an uncredentialled, graphomaniacal paranoic without a book deal.

(DENISE *stands up.*)

DENISE: Let's go inside, Oliver.

OLIVER: An estate lawyer, now there's an honorable profession for the first husband.

DENISE: You couldn't keep working on that book forever. You know that. You'd lose your mind. This is a win-win. I don't understand why this is an issue.

OLIVER: I think you do understand. So long as I'm the only one who has to sacrifice, everything's swell.

DENISE: I'm so close, Oliver. Please don't do this.

OLIVER: No, you're right. The world needs more politicians, fewer artists.

DENISE: Artists create. You accumulate. (*Small beat*) Oliver, you're blessed with a wide angle lens. You see time and history in panorama, much more broadly than I'm capable of. But now... Darling, you're lost in the margins. Please, come back.

You're right, the city needs me. Which means I need you. Which means, yes, Oliver, I am asking for you to sacrifice. For me. For now. (*Small beat*) All I'm asking is that you please not destroy my life for the possibility of finding meaning in yours.
(DENISE *kisses* OLIVER. *Her Blackberry rings. She pulls it out of her bag and looks at the phone.*)

DENISE: I'm sorry, Oliver. I have to—

OLIVER: I'll be in in a minute.

(DENISE *stands, leaving her purse on the stoop next to* OLIVER. *She answers her phone.*)

DENISE: *(On the phone)* Grubman, one second. *(Covering the phone's mouthpiece and speaking to* OLIVER:) Not all endings have to be funerals, Oliver. Bad things end too. Come in soon, okay? *(Into the phone, curtly—this is her at work:)* Grubman, what the hell are you doing calling me this time of night? You better not be trapped under another vending machine. *(She shakes her head and kisses* OLIVER *on the forehead. To him, gesturing to her bag as she walks into the brownstone:)* Would you bring that in for me? *(She exits.)*

(OLIVER *pulls a pack of American Spirit cigarettes out of his pocket, lights one up, and inhales.*)

(*After a puff or two, he reaches his hand into* DENISE's *purse and pulls out her electronic City Hall Security I D badge. He stares at it, turning it over in his hand. Smoke rises from his lit cigarette.*)

Scene Eight

(*Later that night.* TRACY *and* TODD's *hotel room in Times Square. He is lying on the bed with a wet towel over his forehead. He's moaning. She rushes into the room, the door slamming shut behind her.*)

TRACY: Toddie. Kendrick.

TODD: Tracy.

TRACY: Kendrick! You couldn't have been a Manson, or a Dahmer, or a Disney…

TODD: Not now, Tracy…

TRACY: No, you're right. We can wait until tomorrow to discuss how you've lied about every single detail you've shared with me since the day we met. We can wait until tomorrow for you to explain to me how I ended up engaged to the son of the greatest political monster of our generation. We can wait—

TODD: Please, Tracy.

TRACY: No, I'm sorry, Toddie. You don't get to say "please" to me anymore. Why don't you try, "I'm so so sorry, I'll do anything you ask, you're a goddess, I'm a shit."

TODD: Where were you? I waited for you outside the restaurant for half an hour.

(TRACY *goes to her suitcase and begins shoving her clothes into it.)*

TODD: What're you doing?

TRACY: I'm packing. Mostly, Toddie—

TODD: Stop that.

TRACY: *(Still packing)* Mostly, I'm confused. Could you clarify something for me: what did you think was going to happen here? You figured you could sneak off and have dinner with Mommy without me asking any questions? I'm a re-por-ter!

TODD: I was working on it. I had a plan… Or I didn't. I don't know. My head is killing me.

TRACY: Okay, cause I can think of two explanations for your lapse into dumbass-ery. The first—my personal favorite—is that you are incurably deranged.

TODD: Just sit down, Tracy.

TRACY: Are you deranged? It would explain, I mean, just so so much. Now, the other possibility, Toddie, is that, in actuality, you wanted me to find out. About all of this.

TODD: Trust me, I didn't.

TRACY: I'm sorry, I could have sworn you just said "Trust me".

You told me your father was dead.

TODD: He will be soon.

TRACY: But if you were in a lying mood, why didn't you just tell me your mother'd died too? Two birds with one gravestone. / We could have avoided this whole—

TODD: I don't know. I didn't. / Can we talk about this tomorrow?

TRACY: Yes, we can talk about this tomorrow. And the next day and the day after that and on and on until death do us part. But we're also talking about it now.

TODD: So you're not leaving without me?

TRACY: You wish, you little ferret-weasel. Can you try, just attempt to imagine how I—I mean, I finally convince the Dispatch to let me write a feature, and you—stop the presses! —agree to come with, show me where you're from. I was so...I thought maybe this ring finally gave me access to something...more, you know? Yeah, and well, it doesn't take a genius to figure out why, after eight years of refusing to cross the Queensboro Bridge, you chose to do it now. But, I guess, I don't know, I'd been hoping that it might have been on account of me.

I don't like feeling stupid, Todd. And until tonight, I didn't even know your last name. (*More to herself:*) I didn't know your last name...

TODD: I didn't lie about everything.

TRACY: Ah yes, the words every girl longs to hear.

TODD: Tracy, this place is all toxicity and rot. Let's leave. Go back to Saint Louis. Together. Right now. *(He stands up, his head throbs.)* Okay, maybe not right now.

TRACY: You can calm down, Todd, I'm not leaving you. You wanna know why? *(Small beat)* You gave me Ruby's.

TODD: I gave you… When?

TRACY: The name of the restaurant. You told me it was Ruby's. You had to know I'd come.

TODD: I didn't.

(TRACY sits on the bed next to TODD.)

TRACY: You did. You wanted me to find out. And that, my mendacious paramour, is how someday, in the very very distant future, I will be able to forgive you. But before all that, one question. What exactly did you come back to fix?

TODD: I came back because my mother begged.

TRACY: But what happened? All that stuff you made up—the inheritance—all of that was a lie. So it turns out, on top of everything else, I have no clue—no clue—why you left New York eight years ago, why you moved to Saint Louis. *(Beat)* Well?

TODD: What?

TRACY: You gonna tell me?

TODD: Tracy, I didn't come to heal old wounds. I don't want to hear his side of the story. I don't want to hear hers. I just want to go home with you and wait for the cancer to win.

TRACY: Todd, that is a horrible thing to say.

TODD: Yeah, well, one foul turn…

TRACY: Okay, good. What foul turn? *(Small beat)* What about you mother?

TODD: She's…difficult.

TRACY: Well, I loved her.

TODD: All you two did was fight.

TRACY: *(Shoving the last items into her suitcase)* I know. She's great.

TODD: Wait, can you just— Are we leaving or not?

TRACY: We are.

TODD: Good. Thank you.

TRACY: But, kiddo, we're not going to Saint Louis. *(She goes into the bathroom.)*

TODD: Where then…?

TRACY: *(From off)* After you left, the three of us were talking.

TODD: Oh god…

TRACY: *(From off)* Your dad was explaining his illness, and we got to chatting about his, you know, his legacy and what not…

TODD: Jesus, Tracy. What did you do?

(TRACY enters carrying a bag of toiletries. She dumps them in her suitcase.)

TRACY: I pitched him a book. An authorized biography, from the inside out. In depth interviews, life-story kinda stuff. And guess what fiesty scribe is gonna write it?

TODD: How are you possibly going to— How can you write a biography of a man you've called, on more than one occasion, an autocrat, a hypocrite. What happened to "Manhattan's Mussolini?"

TRACY: No, see but that's exactly it. With me, it'll be a real investigation into his politics and into his past.

Including, we can only hope, an item or two about his prodigal, pseudonymitous son.

TODD: You can't do this.

TRACY: I can. And I'm gonna.

TODD: I'm putting my foot down.

TRACY: Yeah, okay.

TODD: I'm not going back to that house.

TRACY: It'll just be a few months—

TODD: Months!

TRACY: —and we'll be back in Saint Louis by fall.

TODD: We can't stay until fall. We've got things to do.

TRACY: As far as I'm concerned, the only thing you've got to do is pray to God I'm as forgiving as I hope I am.

TODD: What about the Dispatch?

TRACY: Screw the Dispatch. This here, this is the sort of work that puts you on the map.

TODD: Like Twitter?

TRACY: Like Profiles in Courage. I'm Teddy goddamn Sorenson! *(She slides* TODD *his suitcase.)* And I'm starting tomorrow.

TODD: You don't know what you're getting yourself into.

TRACY: That's what's exciting, Toddie.

TODD: All I want is to marry you. And live a sweet life, a small life. We can start a family and raise some normal, only occasionally fucked up kids. We won't bother our stupid neighbors, and our stupid neighbors won't bother us. Tracy, we can get a mailbox shaped like a duck and we can put our last name on it. We can be Todd and Tracy Nevelson.

TRACY: I never said I was taking your pseudonym.

TODD: Let's leave. Tonight. Please.

TRACY: We'll stay with them until the fall. Then my masterpiece will be finished and sweet, little, simple, small Saint Louis, here we come. Just you and me. Mister and Mrs…T B D.

Scene Nine

(The same night. DENISE is on the phone in her home.)

DENISE: The fuck you are! You have to pull the story, Joshua… Because it's baseless. Where did you get the tip off?— Okay, fine, I understand that and I'm not asking for a name. But how did you— …Twitter? You're going to take the word of some anonymous tweets over— …That's not a credible source…. No no no, if you run this story, what, Joshua, is every idiot in this whole fucking country going to read scrolling across the bottom of his twenty-five inch flat screen on your pissant "news" network? —Because I want to hear you say it! —You're such a pussy, Joshua, I swear to god.
It's gonna be three words. That's all. "Mayor Kendrick." Colon. "Cancer."… Not colon cancer, you— the punctuation— …Doesn't matter cause you can't run it because it's not true. And if this story does break, I swear to god, Joshua, I will rip out your nut-sack like a shoelace caught in an escalator. *(She hangs up.)* Shit! Shit shit shit. *(She dials her phone and speaks into it.)* It's me—I don't know, Grubman…I said I don't know. Some idiot on Twitter. Do your fucking job! —Because I just got off the phone with Joshua fucking Sanders who told me that you never even called him… Because talking to the press is not my job. It's yours, you fat fuck! —Elliot, I'm sorry… Please don't cry… You're not. You're not fat— Fifteen pounds, huh? —Yeah,

I've heard the points really work…Grubman, would you please do me a favor? Pull yourself together, get on the phone and fucking handle this! *(She hangs up.)* FUUUUUUUUUUUUUUCK!

(DENISE's phone rings.)

DENISE: Fuck.

(DENISE takes a deep breath. The phone rings again.)

(The phone rings again.)

DENISE: Fuck me.

(The phone rings again. DENISE answers.)

DENISE: John, I can explain.

Scene Ten

(The following tweets are either projected or are read by the cast—aside from JOHN—or are presented to the audience in some other clever fashion.)

Just saw the Mayor on the UES at Ruby's. Some guy got drunk, screamed at him and ran out. #celebsighting

Mayor John Kendrick is in our prayers. @MayorJKendrick

#mayor check out this video i took tonite at dinner with my parents: youtube.com/kipgregory420 dude is crazy #eatyourdamnpasta

We love you, Mayor Kendrick. We're thinking about you. #kendrickhealth

R these rumors true? #kendrickhealth.

This video = nuts. John Kendrick gets screamed at in public! #eatyourdamnpasta

He should be ashamed of himself… #teamkendrick

#eatyourdamnpasta Someone should kick that guy's ass. We love you, Mayor Kendrick @MayorJKendrick

BREAKING NEWS: Mayor Kendrick reported ill with life-threatening disease. More details to come.

Anyone know what's wrong with Kendrick? #kendrickhealth

praying for you @MayorJKendrick

in our thoughts @MayorJKendrick

you beat the Derelicts, you can beat cancer!

someone tell me if this video is real or a hoax—if it's a hoax, not funny! #eatyourdamnpasta

can't believe it's true. #kendrickhealth

"don't go, mayor Kendrick!"

Tell me it's not happening. #kendrickhealth

Pray for the Mayor. Pray for New York.

This St. Louis girl's hitting the big time. More news tomorrow... #lemonslemonade

Scene Eleven

(Continued from Scene Nine. DENISE and JOHN are on the phone, she in her home, he in his home office in Gracie Mansion. He sips from a glass of water throughout.)

DENISE: I'm firing Grubman.

JOHN: You don't have to—

DENISE: No, I am. He's useless and he's gone.

JOHN: That's your decision.

DENISE: And I just whipped up a statement about these health rumors. I can have someone fax it over tonight for your approval. We can get the cameras in first thing tomorrow. It's your run of the mill deny deny deny with a little sidebar about the cowardice of anonymity.

Get some good sound bites about the erosion of human respect and interaction in the Internet Age. You'll sound smart but not smug. And if I do say so myself, you make some solid points, too, without coming across as too much of a Luddite.

JOHN: But it's true.

DENISE: Just because you think Google is a noodle casserole Jews eat on Rosh Hashanah doesn't make you a Luddite.

JOHN: But I do have cancer. What is there to deny?

DENISE: If you confirm that you're… There could be massive panic. Especially right on the heels of the Derelicts' threat.

JOHN: But I have no choice. They'll find out sooner or later.

DENISE: That is a choice. Choose later. Right now, we need your full focus on maintaining order as we handle the threat. John, you've been warning us about this moment for twelve years. The city needs you to follow through on what you'd promised them. After this is all done, then we can tell them you're— We can reveal whatever information we need.

JOHN: After…

(Awkward silence)

DENISE: John, are you… How are you feeling? Or— We don't have to— *(Talk about this)*

JOHN: No, it's fine. It's fine.
I'm tired. I'm never hungry. Helen's had to poke new holes in all my belts. She's already set up a private room in Bellevue—very discreet—in case of an emergency. My neck feels like it's swollen to the size of a football. There's a rash on my chest that won't stop itching. Not to mention this wig.

DENISE: You and your hair.

JOHN: It's a politician's greatest asset.
I'm weak. I'm tired. Did I already say— My knees
ache. My back aches. My legs— Everything. It's spread
to the spleen—or rather, not spread. It's appeared in
the spleen. N H L—the, uh, Non-Hodgkin's, uh— *(He
coughs.)*

DENISE: Uh huh.

JOHN: It doesn't always metastasize to adjacent—
Since it's a cancer of white blood cells, of the immune
system, it can really sprout up anywhere.

DENISE: Like weeds.

JOHN: Or high-rise condos. Started in the lymph nodes,
now it's in my bone marrow. It's in my spleen. What a
way to go, huh? Ironic, almost…

DENISE: Ironic?

JOHN: The immune system, the very thing programmed
to keep this machine—me—going, is the thing that's
going to kill me.

DENISE: Are you sure you're comfortable talking about
this? We don't have to—

JOHN: No no. I don't mind.

DENISE: You're okay discussing it?

JOHN: Sure.

DENISE: Good.

JOHN: Good.

(Silence)

DENISE: Well, now I don't have anything to say.

JOHN: Then let's get off the topic of my insurgent white
blood cells and onto business. This threat…

DENISE: Right.

JOHN: You've released the letter to the Times?

DENISE: Should be in print and on the site tomorrow morning.

JOHN: Good.

DENISE: And I've got a meeting with the Twitter people tomorrow, see if there's any way they'll give me contact information for whoever posted the first video.

JOHN: No need. What's happened happened.

DENISE: Have you spoken with Todd about this yet? If I were you, I'd be pretty fucking furious. I've got a cousin in the I R S. Just say the word—

JOHN: Thanks for the offer, but it's not his fault. He didn't— *(He stops. Deep breath)*

DENISE: John, are you—

JOHN: He brought his fiancee home. Bright girl. Very... sprited.

DENISE: Always so polite.

JOHN: She's a journalist. Going to write a biography of me.

DENISE: Now? John, don't you think there are other things you should be focusing on?

JOHN: Someone's got to keep a record of how incredibly charming and heroic and handsome Mayor John Kendrick was in his day. *(He laughs, then coughs.)*

DENISE: Is she any good?

JOHN: I don't know. But she and Todd are staying. Until she's finished.

DENISE: I see.

JOHN: What else is on the docket for tomorrow?

DENISE: Well, after Twitter, I'm running down to the big three networks, see if I can convince them to play up the threat, play down the illness.
So, this statement, the statement denying your, uh...

JOHN: Yes.

DENISE: You're sure you don't want to give it.

JOHN: I'm sure. In fact, let's schedule another fireside for tomorrow evening.

DENISE: And in the meantime, the newspeople're going to ask me about your health. What do you want me to say?

JOHN: Tell them the truth. That's what we tell them when they ask. The truth.

Scene Twelve

Tuesday, July 7

(The next morning. TODD sits in his parent's home, reading a copy of The New York Times. *He reads aloud. He is quizzical at first, but as he reads, he becomes increasingly mesmerized.)*

TODD: "Dated July Fourth.
Dear Mayor John Kendrick, Dear People of the City of New York, Dear Puppet, Dear Puppet Master, Dear America,
A Warning:
Watch. A master craftsman carves from a single block of wood a work of art—the body of a marionette. Picked and sawed and chipped and sanded, a rough-hewn branch born of a sturdy oak or birch succumbs to artistry, to progress. And in such supple supplication becomes a thing of beauty. A finger dragged across the puppet's chest above his heart, were hollowed wood a hold for beating organs, yields not a single splinter nor

any sign of error on the craftsman's part. The body is
perfection.

But look, America, upon the ground at the master's
feet. There find the remnants of this block of wood—
the sacrifices made in search of orderly perfection.

And watch, Land of Liberty, as the master takes up the
broom and, with a whistle or a sigh, removes offending
excess.

See the master now wrap his fingers round a cross
and make the puppet dance. In dancing, you forget
the excess. You forget the sacrifice that made wood
smooth. You forget, America, what was lost in pursuit
of a body perfect.

Still, look within. Still, the puppet rots. Still, maggots
and termites devour his heartless breast. He will be no
more. Excess wood and puppet then as one, America,
at the wind's whim.

The day comes soon, New York. Destruction from
within. Destruction, wrapped in corruption, wrapped
in government, in a palace of stone. Torturous,
burning, slow death to you, New York. It begins at City
Hall.

There is no hope.

Yours,

The Derelicts Forgotten."

Scene Thirteen

(*The same day. Outside City Hall,* OLIVER *smokes a
cigarette and stares out at a large crowd of people who have
gathered outside the building. He is clearly troubled.*)

(TRACY *enters and approaches* OLIVER.)

TRACY: Sorry to bother you, but do you think I could
bum a light?

OLIVER: Oh. Uh… Sure.

(OLIVER *ignites a lighter and lights* TRACY'S *cigarette.*)

TRACY: Thanks. *(She exhales, a little nervous.)* God,
would you look at all these people.
Has it been like this all day?

OLIVER: I got here a few hours ago. Crowd was half
this size.

TRACY: Jesus, doubled in a few hours... What are they
doing?

OLIVER: They've been leaving flowers, cards, carrying
candles. I've heard prayers, I've heard tears.

TRACY: A vigil.

OLIVER: Guess so.

TRACY: I've been following this on Twitter. People are
spreading the word to gather here, but I had no idea
it'd be this...I mean, wow.
You work in City Hall?

OLIVER: No. No, I was doing research.

TRACY: Yeah, me too. Actually, I'm interviewing the
Mayor today. Which is pretty, you know, it's big.
I'm nervous, kind of, I think, but it could be a chance
to really— I mean, make a difference, you know?
Could be something big. *(Small beat)* I'm writing his
authorized biography, actually, so...

(Small beat, OLIVER'S *lost in thought.)*

TRACY: Trust me, I'm the first one to criticize the guy.
Actually, last night, I was having dinner with him, at
Ruby's on the Upper East Side, and—not to toot my
own—whatever but, I sort of took him to school. Yeah,
he's done some questionable things, sure, but, like—I
guess that's what I'm digging into in this book. How
does he justify his actions, not just to the city, but to
himself. This could be—I don't want to get ahead of

myself. I mean, it could be pretty…I don't even want to jinx it.

What did you say you were researching?

OLIVER: A, uh, a book.

TRACY: A fellow wordsmith. What's the future bestseller about?

OLIVER: *(Gesturing to the gathering crowd)* Them. I'm writing about this.

TRACY: About the vigil? Sorry, I don't think I…

OLIVER: My work's in history. And we're on the verge of the historic. All this adoration isn't grief, it's terror. As he decays, so decays the barrier between them and their worst fear.

TRACY: What, the Derelicts?

OLIVER: Responsibility. How much easier is it to be afraid than burdened?

TRACY: Well hot damn. That is some pretty dour hypothesizing.

OLIVER: What is history except a litary of wounds; unhealed and festering? An infection spreading through time, impossible to stop, impossible to cure.

TRACY: Okay then. Yeah, so I should probably head inside.

OLIVER: I'm sorry. I know how I must… You know, I think I used to be an optimist.

TRACY: Hey, I get it. Dark times.

(Small beat)

OLIVER: Do you ever wish you weren't right?

TRACY: Me? No.

OLIVER: I do. Almost every day.

TRACY: And are you? Wrong?

OLIVER: Sadly, I am not.

TRACY: Well, you're writing a book. You damn well better be right. It's your job to tell the truth. Everything else is garnish.

OLIVER: What about the cost?

TRACY: The truth, I think, no matter what, is what's best for the common good.

(OLIVER *smiles.*)

OLIVER: The common good. I like that.

TRACY: What?

OLIVER: Why would what's good for you be what's good for me? There really isn't anything common about it.

(OLIVER *stares out into the crowd.* TRACY *takes a drag and follows his gaze.*)

(*Up in Riverside Park,* HELEN *and* TODD *stroll over to a bench in the shadow of Grant's Tomb.*)

TODD: Don't they have jobs? Places to be?

HELEN: They do. But they love your father.

TODD: No, they worship him.

TRACY: All this for one guy. We should all be so lucky. (*Beat*) I don't know what it is you've got on your hands right now, and I'm sure it's... Some things, maybe, are bigger than us. Maybe sometimes the only way to view the world is from above.

HELEN: He's helped this city through one of its darkest times. The gathering outside City Hall today, that's merely reciprocation.

TODD: But that they're all there together. It's like this feeling's spread. Like a virus.

(TRACY *takes a final puff, tosses the cigarette on the ground and puts it out with her foot.*)

TRACY: I should head in. I've got tea with Mussolini. Thanks for the light.

(TRACY *walks into the building.* OLIVER *stares at the crowd.*)

HELEN: Toddie, you'll never get anywhere thinking of them as rational, individual citizens. A single person is rational, yes. An individual makes choices, thinks. But to govern you need to understand that a citizenry, it acts as one.

TODD: You do know how condescending you sound, don't you?

HELEN: I'm helping you to understand what you're father's done these last—

TODD: (*Not wanting to talk about his father*) You're talking about them like they're some mindless mob.

HELEN: Not mindless. Unified.

TODD: Right. And the city's just one big bee hive.

(HELEN *chuckles.*)

HELEN: Well, that may be the greatest thing your father's done. He's unified the disparate.

(*Beat*)

(OLIVER *puts out his cigarette, exits.*)

TODD: So, why did you want to come all the way up here, mother?

HELEN: Grant's Tomb.

TODD: Yeah. It's…a tomb.

HELEN: Your father and I used to relax here for hours. He'd give ranting lectures to the trees and to the river about the future. His future, he called it, as if his breath were the engine that spun the globe. We'd talk about everything then. His hopes for this city. For you.

TODD: And is this what he'd hoped?

HELEN: I'm glad you're staying, Toddie.

TODD: Not by choice. This is important to Tracy, but once the book is finished, we're leaving.

HELEN: Your father talks about you quite a bit.

TODD: Does he?

HELEN: He asks me what you're doing.

TODD: Teaching middle school?

HELEN: No. From time to time, at dinner or while he's reading in bed or when we're walking through the park, out of the blue, his eyes will lose focus and he'll tilt his head to one side and he'll ask, "What is Toddie doing right now?" He asks as if I know the answer.

TODD: I'm not going to forgive him. That's not why I'm here.

HELEN: But you are here.

TODD: For now.

HELEN: For now.

(HELEN *and* TODD *look up at the tomb.*)

HELEN: Toddie, do you know where the word mausoleum comes from?

TODD: It is so incredibly hot. Can we—

HELEN: The word originates with Queen Artemisia of Halicarnassus.

TODD: Etymology? Now? Really?

HELEN: I just finished this really fantastic biography. It's got a great ending. Really… Well, she was one of the rare militarily-savvy ancient queens of Asia Minor. She and her husband Mausolus built an incredible city together. They spared nothing, no expense to show the whole world how well-off they were.

TODD: Ah, so they were Upper East Siders too.

HELEN: When her husband died, she built him a great tomb.

TODD: Mausolus, like mausoleum. Got it. So, should we head back or—

HELEN: It was almost a hundred fifty feet tall, sparkling white, and adorned with the finest sculptures crafted by the city's most skilled artists. When it was finally complete, Artemisia, the warrior-queen, took her husband's ashes and lay them at the heart of the great stone monument. What better gift could she give her husband than a place in history? The tomb of Mausolus, one of the seven wonders of the ancient world.
She lived two more years. And when she died, her ashes were placed right alongside her husband's.
It really is a great ending.

(HELEN *and* TODD *both look up at Grant's Tomb.*)

HELEN: Grant's wife Julia is buried there beside him. Isn't it remarkable? It's…Gotham's Giza.

TODD: It looks like a giant orange juicer.

HELEN: *(Smiling)* It does.
A great man deserves a great monument, Toddie.

TODD: That why you got Tracy to write that book?

HELEN: It was her idea.

TODD: Was it? You know, it's not going to be the spit-shined hagiography you were hoping for. She's critical. And smart.

HELEN: He's persuasive when he knows he's right.

TODD: I remember.

HELEN: But regardless, she can write whatever she wants. It's her book.

TODD: You don't care what she says?

HELEN: Her little tome won't carve his name in stone. History'll do that for us all. At least, those with names worth carving.

TODD: You know, Grant was, in many ways, a monster. And he was a terrible president. He—

HELEN: When you leave here, what will you do?

TODD: Go home. Teach. Get married.

HELEN: And then?

TODD: That's life, Mother. The "and then"…

(HELEN *stares at* TODD. *A long beat*)

TODD: What?

HELEN: I thought time might have… Ah well. The pipe dreams of the old and hopeful.
If you're going to go, go now.

TODD: Tracy just started. The book's going to take months, at least.

HELEN: You came—

TODD: Because you asked!

HELEN: And I'm grateful. But I was mistaken. Go home, Toddie. There's not much time left.

TODD: I'm not doing this with you, Mother. We agreed not to talk about him.

HELEN: Not your father. He'll go when he's ready, not a breath before. No, I'm not concerned about him.

TODD: You really want me to go. After all the— You know what? Fine. If you don't want me here, great. I... We'll go. Shouldn't have come to begin with. *(He goes to leave, stops, turns back.)* There's not much time left for me, is that what you're saying? Because I'm going to be fine. Maybe even happy, maybe. Which is more than I can say for... Not everybody wants to be buried in a pyramid.

(HELEN shakes her head.)

HELEN: Toddie, what happens when you bat at a hive? The trouble isn't the thousand bees you must contend with. It's the swarm.

Go home, Toddie. Go home.

(HELEN walks away leaving TODD staring up at the tomb.)

Scene Fourteen

(The same day, in JOHN's office in City Hall. He is sitting in an armchair, drinking from his water glass. TRACY, taking notes, sits alongside him.)

TRACY: And your father—how long was he in office?

JOHN: One and a half terms. He died in the third year of his last term. Congenital heart failure.

TRACY: Yes, I read that somewhere online. Wikipedia, maybe, so who knows if it's true.

JOHN: I do. I watched him die.

TRACY: Oh—I'm—I'm sorry, I wasn't implying that—

JOHN: It was remarkable. Like someone reached inside him and pulled a cord. Like a lamp. His eyes just sort of *(He snaps.)* turned off. And all that was left was a lampshade. It was very educational.

TRACY: That must have been awful.

JOHN: I was the only one with him. He turned to me and he looked into my eyes with a tractor beam stare, and he said "Johnny, follow in my footsteps. Dedicate your life to leading this city to greatness as I did mine."

TRACY: Oh my god.

(Beat)

JOHN: No, that's not true. But wouldn't that have been something? No, he muttered something I couldn't understand and then kind of gasped, and that was it. Such is death. You can live pretty, but I don't care who you are, you sure as hell don't die pretty. You die dead.

TRACY: That's awfully pessimistic, don't you think?

JOHN: It's the truth. When I go, I can tell you one thing. It ain't gonna be pretty.

(There's a noise from outside—a siren and the roar of a crowd. TRACY goes to the window. JOHN takes the opportunity to drink his water. He leans back, clutches his left side and breathes deeply.)

TRACY: The crowd's still growing. There must be five, six hundred people out there.

JOHN: My father…

TRACY: Are you not fazed by this? This is all for you, you know.

JOHN: They're doing this for their own sake, to help them cope with something they don't think they understand. It's not for me.

TRACY: John, I don't—

JOHN: My father…

TRACY: *(Sitting back down)* Your father…was the reason you went into politics?

JOHN: I wanted to be a lawyer, honestly. I was up in Boston for law school. When I was starting my own practice, I knew I wanted to move back down to New York City. To raise children. You gonna have kids?

TRACY: I don't… Yes. Someday.

JOHN: My grandkids.

TRACY: Yeah.

(Small beat)

JOHN: Back then, I was a corporate shill. In it for the buck. "All these— All the meanness and agony without end, I sitting, look out upon, See, hear, and am silent." You know it?

TRACY: I don't.

JOHN: Whitman. *Leaves of Grass.* You like Whitman?

TRACY: Doesn't everybody?

JOHN: Oh, I do. A true American Humanist. "See, hear and am silent." That was me.
It took me a long time to understand my father. At first I hated everything he stood for. I argued with him constantly. He would do—I didn't understand what he was doing. Take the Lower Manhattan Conservancy Initiative.

TRACY: I'm sorry, I'm not familiar…

JOHN: The L M C I was a vestigial line item in the budget. For the life of me I can't recall what the money was originally allocated for. Maybe it was a typo. But whatever it was, my father— *(He winces slightly and puts his hand on his side.)*

TRACY: John, are you—

JOHN: *(Waving her off)* —he caught the mistake. He knew that extra money was there, but he never asked anyone to remove it from the budget. When he submitted his new budget each year, he left it in.

TRACY: Why wouldn't he just correct the error?

JOHN: Because he used the money.

TRACY: You're telling me he stole from the taxpayers?

JOHN: No, you're not seeing the big picture, Tracy. He didn't use it on himself. But because he didn't have to go through the whole three-ring circus—the committees, the councils, the bureaucracy—he could use the money where and when the city needed it most. At his discretion.

TRACY: But, John, technically, that's a crime.

JOHN: Perhaps. But victimless.

TRACY: What about the taxpayer?

JOHN: *(Sometimes pained, but he speaks through, making a point)* To them, government is alchemy. As long as they've got gold in the end, the transformation's of no interest.
When my father first told me about it, he thought it was something I should hear. But he was wrong. It wasn't until many, many years later that I understood. It wasn't until I had the proper perspective.
Sometimes, it takes what it takes.

TRACY: So, to hell with the process, then? Screw the system?

JOHN: Governing is the act of betterment tempered by discussion. In the end, the city was a better place. That's what people remember. That's the legacy.

TRACY: All right, then what do you think your legacy is going to be?

JOHN: I don't know, Tracy. You tell me.

Scene Fifteen

(That night. OLIVER *is seated at his kitchen table, across which are strewn notebooks, paper and newspapers. He's pouring over the items on the table when* DENISE *enters, hurried.)*

DENISE: Okay, sorry, meetings all day, but I've got to run down to City Hall. The Mayor's doing another fireside tonight about his health and about the Derelicts and— I'm just grabbing a bite. Did the firm call today? They said they'd call? *(Beat)* Oliver? Did the firm call? *(She notices the mess on the table.)* What's all this?

OLIVER: Denise...

DENISE: No, I can't do this right now. Oliver, we were done with this!

OLIVER: I need to ask you a question.

DENISE: Not now. But believe me, we will discuss this later. Right now, I have to get down to City Hall.

OLIVER: You might need this to get in. *(He holds up her security badge.)*

DENISE: Where did—Oliver. What did you do?

OLIVER: I have to ask you a question, Denise.

DENISE: After we specifically discussed— / Oliver!

OLIVER: I need to know if you—

DENISE: Jesus Christ, do you know what this could mean for me!? You may have just single-handedly destroyed my political career before it even began. If anyone knew that you—that I—How could you take this kind of risk?
Did anybody see?

OLIVER: Aren't you the least bit curious what I found?

DENISE: No, Oliver! I'm not. You lied to me. Did anybody see? *(Small beat)* Give me the— *(She snatches the security badge from him.)* When I get back tonight, you're going to give me a list of every single guard, every janitor, every fucking pigeon who saw you go in, who saw you go out. You are going to—

OLIVER: Eight-hundred forty-three.

DENISE: Eight-hundred forty-three what?

OLIVER: That's how many I counted. There may be more. Did you know about this?

DENISE: What are you talking about, Oliver?

OLIVER: If you were a part of this, I need to know now. Because once it's in print, there's no undoing what's been done.

DENISE: I can't believe you're— Now, of all times, now, you—
Okay, what? Tell me what you're talking about and I can tell you what I know.

OLIVER: When the administration—when Kendrick's new branch of the N Y P D rounds up someone they believe might be a Derelict, they bring them before a panel.

DENISE: Yes, Oliver. Everyone knows that.

OLIVER: These panels are still operating.

DENISE: That's public knowledge. They're operating to maintain a cap on the Derelict threat. Like what happened this week, for instance. Oliver, what are you talking about?

OLIVER: According to what I found, Denise, Kendrick would have these homeless paraded out, one by one—

DENISE: *(Concurrent with below)* Paraded. If you're going to be melodramatic, I'm not—

OLIVER: *(Concurrent with above)* The panels would investigate a suspect's family, his background. Yes, most of the homeless were cleared and placed in programs, privatized shelters. Which is exactly what everyone thinks has been happening.
But another pattern appears over and over again in the transcripts.

DENISE: What pattern, Oliver? What transcripts?

OLIVER: I was looking through the basement files, digging for memos, meeting minutes, trying to find something concrete for *The Chronicle*—

DENISE: *(Concurrent with below)* You mean doing exactly what I told you not to do!

OLIVER: *(Concurrent with above)* And amongst all these files, I found a crate. An unlabeled crate full of testimonies. They started twelve years ago, but the most recent—and who knows how many other crates there are—was a transcript from last year. Last year, Denise. So I'm asking, did you know about this?

DENISE: Oliver, I don't know what you're talking about.

OLIVER: Of the thousands who've been questioned, at least eight-hundred forty-three people came before the panels with no evidence linking them in any way with any violent activity and, without a trial, without a jury, without a judge, were incarcerated.

DENISE: Yeah, that can't be true, Oliver. You must have misunderstood. Forgetting about the massive legal issues in play, I mean, what reason would the administration possibly have for doing that? It's ludicrous.

OLIVER: Homelessness destroys the illusion of security. "If it can happen to that guy, it could happen to you." Not to mention crime, cleanliness, quiet. For Kendrick to maintain his power—

DENISE: *(Overlapping with below)* Okay, Oliver, you're scaring me.

OLIVER: *(Overlapping with above)* —he needs to prove that he's made a difference, made the city safer. So, if some innocent man is unlucky enough to come across a police officer, if he has no family, no education, if he's sick, if he could be a potential blemish on the white washed facade of this city, if the amount of money or effort required to incorporate him into society outweighs the cost of—

DENISE: Do you know how much it costs to keep someone in prison?

OLIVER: Yes, but that's the wrong question. The real question is how much the illusion is worth. When your entire governing policy's built on the guarantee of safety, wouldn't you spend any amount of money to keep that promise? Shelters don't have bars. You can't force these people out of sight. Unless…

DENISE: If what you're saying is true…

OLIVER: I'm telling you, eight-hundred forty-three innocent people were incarcerated. Eight-hundred forty-three sentences with Kendrick's signature. Eight-hundred forty-three homeless men and women deemed irreclaimable and banished to a prison cell, some for life, for the crime of being…what? Hopeless? Sick? Alone? *(Small beat)* This is it. This is what was missing from *The Chronicle*.

DENISE: If you put this nonsense into a manuscript and anybody, some intern in the Random House mailroom even, sees it, that is it. I will lose my job.

Do you want to do this because it could help people or because it'd sell your book?

OLIVER: Why does there have to be a difference?

DENISE: Whatever it is you think you found, Oliver, you didn't. If this were true, I would know.

OLIVER: I have to go back, take photos of the transcripts. Tomorrow, come with me into the basement. Let me show you.

DENISE: No, Oliver. I'm not risking anyone seeing you nosing around in classified files.

OLIVER: Then go without me. See for yourself.

DENISE: If even any small part of what you said is real—

OLIVER: So you believe me—

DENISE: I said if. And no. And electronic security records can be subpoenaed. I need to maintain plausible deniability. And you can't go back, are you fucking kidding me?

OLIVER: We have to tell the people this is happening. You have to believe me, Denise.

DENISE: I believe that you think you found something. But I also believe you know what this would do to my career, and I think you're lashing out at me— *(Continue below)*

OLIVER: *(Concurrent with below)* That's not what's happening—

DENISE: *(Concurrent with above)* —I think you're lashing out at me and I think that this is a vindictive and childish and ill-advised maneuver to destroy my future because you have this misguided belief that somehow I've destroyed yours.

OLIVER: This has nothing do with us! This isn't even about *The Chronicle* anymore.

DENISE: *(Concurrent with below)* Which you put to rest! You told me you were done! I'm concerned—

OLIVER: *(Concurrent with above)* Don't you understand, Denise, these are human lives we're talking about! People are still in prison. We could get them out.

DENISE: I don't know what's happened to you these last few years. What this book has done to you. I don't know where you went. But I'm not going to let you pull me down there with you.
I don't think I can—I don't think I can be near you right now.

OLIVER: Denise, please... Listen.

DENISE: No, Oliver, there has to be a line.
I don't know what's going to happen next, Oliver, but right now, I have to go.

(DENISE turns to leave. OLIVER grabs her arm.)

OLIVER: Please trust me.

(DENISE tries to shake OLIVER off. He won't let go.)

OLIVER: I'm your husband.

DENISE: Let go!

(OLIVER's squeezing DENISE's arm, shaking her. It's scary.)

OLIVER: *(Concurrent with below)* I'm not fabricating this. I'm not imagining it. This happened, is still happening, and you have to trust me.

DENISE: *(Concurrent with above)* Let go of me, Oliver. You're hurting my... Ow. Oliver!
Let me go!!

(OLIVER lets DENISE go and takes a step back.)

OLIVER: What can I do to make you believe me?

DENISE: If you try to reach those files again, if you even try to get past the front door of City Hall, I will have you arrested.

OLIVER: Denise…

DENISE: I'm not giving up my life for you, Oliver. I won't.

Scene Sixteen

(Bright lights illuminate JOHN, *seated in his plush arm chair, sipping his iced tea.)*

JOHN: Good evening, my fellow New Yorkers. This week has been a week of tests. Much has been asked of you this week, and, as I knew you would, you have risen to the challenge. After all, this is New York City. *(He chuckles, it turns into a cough.)* To those who have gathered here, outside the steps of City Hall, I thank you for your thoughts and for your wishes.
As you by now are certainly aware, my health has been declining for some time. But I assure you, I will expend my every breath to the very last defending you, my fellow New Yorkers, from any threat that may come your way. *(He feels a sharp pain in his back, on the left side, but he does his best not to let it show.)* Together, as one, we will survive the crashing waves and make it home to shore.

*(*TRACY *in a bedroom in Gracie Mansion. She's got a notepad and pen on her lap.* TODD *comes in with a suitcase and shuts off the T V.)*

TRACY: Hey!

TODD: Tracy…

TRACY: Turn it back on. Your dad's speech.

TODD: Tracy, we have to leave.

TRACY: Not now, I need to hear this. Somehow, it's weird, somehow watching him talk, he actually makes you feel like it's gonna be okay, you know? I mean, he's good.

TODD: Please, Tracy. We have to go.

(TRACY *turns to* TODD, *sees the suitcase.*)

TRACY: Where are we going...?

TODD: Saint Louis. I booked us tickets but we have to leave now.

TRACY: Todd, I'm not leaving. I just started today. Why would we go?

TODD: You don't understand how much the people of this city rely on him. He's not just their leader, he's their...

TRACY: Their father? Good, see, this is a good start. Sort of Freudian, but good good. That's progress. Why don't you talk to him tomorrow?

TODD: They won't know what to do when they hear him say he's leaving them.

TRACY: They won't, or...

TODD: Something going to happen, something...

TRACY: What?

TODD: I don't know.
A swarm.

(OLIVER, *at his table, reads over notes he took on transcripts.*)

OLIVER: "Chairman: Are you aware that perjury before this panel is punishable with a sentence as high as life in prison?

Browning: I am sir. But I'm not lying. I don't know nobody who's ever met a Derelict.

Chairman: We will consider your case and render a verdict presently." *(He digs through papers and comes across another document.)* Browing...Browning... "30 to life." Jesus.

JOHN: *(His breathing is slightly more strained)* It's times such as these that a citizenry must prove its mettle. Powerful questions have been asked of you in these moments, these cloudy days. And a powerful question demands a forceful answer. *(He winces, he grabs his side and holds it as he carries on.)* So, will we be a city of individuals who crumble under pressure? Will we be broken by the forces pushing on us now from all sides?

TRACY: A swarm, Todd? What's the matter with you?

TODD: It's not too late to leave. But we have to go now.

TRACY: Okay, I really don't like this. You're making me— Okay, like, I feel like I don't have a choice in anything right now, you're making me feel pressured, but if this is going to be a partnership then—

TODD: We can talk about this on the way, I promise, but please...

TRACY: I'm not giving up the biggest opportunity of my entire life because you're afraid people are going to be sad about your dad. I'm not.

TODD: You don't understand what's about to happen.

TRACY: Oh, and you do?

(JOHN rises his to his feet. The action is slow and painful, but somehow triumphant.)

JOHN: Or will we stand up, will we raise our voices and will we shout "No more!" "No more!"
Will we stare fear in its fiery eyes and demand, "This city will carry on! This city will thrive and we will live! Violence and sickness and death cannot, will not break our backs!" *(He winces again, in pain.)*

OLIVER: "Chairmen: Do you have any family members? Any next of kin?"

(JOHN is bombastic now, nearly shouting.)

JOHN: And though we fear what lies before us on our journey, tomorrow looms large, not as a shadow, but as a window toward something greater—the future. *(Cough)* Your future, a future full of— *(Cough)* Full—

(JOHN winces, then collapses on the ground. DENISE rushes to him.)

TODD: They think he's infallible, he's their great protector.

(TODD's phone rings. He ignores it.)

TODD: And when they know he's sick, it'll get even worse. He'll be a saint, a martyr. Please, let's—

TRACY: Todd, you're getting flushed. Sit down for second or take a—

(The phone rings again.)

TRACY: Answer it.

(Scenes overlap, building to a cacophony. The following occurs concurrent with the scenes below:)

DENISE: John, are you okay? John! John! Can you hear me? Will somebody call an ambulance? Somebody call a—John!
Would you turn off that camera? I said turn off the fucking camera!

(We hear the sound of a siren growing louder. The crowd outside the building is in a frenzy.)

DENISE: John, are you awake? Can you hear me? Just keep breathing— Fuck. It's gonna be okay John. You're going to be okay. Fuck! Fucking Fuck!

OLIVER: *(Concurrent with above and below)* "Chairman: Do you have any next of kin?
Are you married? ...Employment status?
This is your third appearance before the panel...
How long have you lived without a home?...
Are you or have you even been in collusion with the Derelicts?
I have not.
Are you or have you even been in collusion with the Derelicts?
No.
Are you or have you even been in collusion with the Derelicts?
No."

(The following occurs concurrent with OLIVER above:)

TODD: *(On the phone)* Hello? —What do you mean collapsed? *(To TRACY:)* Tracy, turn on the T V.

TRACY: Todd, what's wrong?

TODD: Turn on the goddamn T V!

(TRACY does.)

NEWSREPORTER: *(On the T V, under the rest of the scene)*
—collapsed unexpectedly a moment ago. As you can
see, he's being attended to, but the ambulance hasn't
arrived yet. The crowd outside City Hall is pushing
toward the door, trampling over people to get there.
It's turning into a riot situation out here—

TRACY: Oh my god, Todd!

TODD: Dad!

TRACY: Todd, what do we— Oh my god.

*(Suddenly, the chaos stops. Everything goes dark and silent,
aside from* HELEN, *alone, talking on her phone, in a single
light.)*

HELEN: Take him to Bellevue. I'll be right there.

(Blackout)

END OF ACT ONE

An Entr'acte

*(Some time after ACT ONE. OLIVER sits at a table at the
center of a vast darkness. A bright light illuminates his
worried face, his day-old clothes, and his bound hands.)*

*(The voices of the four INTERROGATORS emanate from the
darkness.)*

FIRST INTERROGATOR: Your name.

OLIVER: Oliver Judd.

FIRST INTERROGATOR: Your full name.

OLIVER: Oliver Judd. I don't have a middle name.

SECOND INTERROGATOR: Place of residence?

OLIVER: 68 Perry Street. New York, New York. 10014.

SECOND INTERROGATOR: Employment status.

OLIVER: I'm a writer.

SECOND INTERROGATOR: This is your profession?

OLIVER: Well, I haven't made any so-called profit from
it as yet, per se. But yes.

FIRST INTERROGATOR: I'm unclear. Are you or are you
not a professional writer?

OLIVER: Aspiring.

SECOND INTERROGATOR: Put down unemployed.

THIRD INTERROGATOR: Do you have any family
members? Any next of kin?

OLIVER: *(Very eagerly)* Yes. Yes. I, uh, I have a wife. I'm married. Denise Powell. She's the First Deputy Mayor. If you call her, she can tell you / that this is all—

FIRST INTERROGATOR: This is the same Denise Powell who alerted City Hall Security of your presence in restricted areas of said building?

OLIVER: I didn't… I wasn't aware of that. I couldn't say.

FOURTH INTERROGATOR: Are you or have you ever been in collusion with the Derelicts?

OLIVER: No sir.

FIRST INTERROGATOR: Are you aware that perjury before this panel is punishable with a sentence as high as life in prison?

OLIVER: I am, sir. But I'm not lying. I haven't done anything wrong.

THIRD INTERROGATOR: Did you not, on more than one occasion, access classified documents you found in the basement of City Hall?

OLIVER: I did not.

FIRST INTERROGATOR: Are you aware that perjury before this panel is—

OLIVER: Yes. I may have taken a small peek at some files. A glance, really. But I didn't see anything. I promise.

FOURTH INTERROGATOR: We will consider your file. You will be hearing from us shortly.

OLIVER: That's it? Isn't there a jury? Or a judge I can stand before to plead my—

THIRD INTERROGATOR: For purposes of security, this panel exists outside the bounds of the Federal or State Judicial System.

SECOND INTERROGATOR: We have been selected for our impartiality

FOURTH INTERROGATOR: Discretion

THIRD INTERROGATOR: Expertise

FIRST INTERROGATOR: And people skills.

FOURTH INTERROGATOR: You will be hearing from us shortly.

OLIVER: That's all?

FOURTH INTERROGATOR: In the meantime you will be provided comfortable lodging in the basement of the Manhattan Municipal Building adjacent to City Hall. As a precaution, you will not be allowed visitors of any kind. Your location will remain undisclosed to protect your safety as well as the safety of the city.

OLIVER: For how long? When can I— / What about Habeus Corpus? What about a trial by jury, the Sixth Amendment!?

FOURTH INTERROGATOR: Henceforth, all decisions related to your incarceration, as well as your as yet undetermined collusion with the Derelict threat will be the sole purview of the panel, subject only to override by the Mayor directly.

OLIVER: You can't do this to me. You can't do this!

FIRST INTERROGATOR: We can assure you, Mr Judd, if you are free of guilt, you have absolutely no reason for concern.

ACT TWO

Scene One

(The following tweets are either projected or are read by the cast—aside from JOHN*—or are presented to the audience in some other clever fashion. All Tweets containing the hashtag "#kendrickupdate" come from* TRACY*'s Twitter account.)*

"The infection in his spleen is under control. His condition is stable. More updates soon #kendrickupdate

Last night at City Hall was epic. Come join us again to remember and support a great man #collectivemourning

Mayor Kendrick is awake. According to Doctors he's recovering remarkably well. More info to come. #kendrickupdate

thx @TracyHols for the updates. love to the family, prayers for @MayorJKendrick

Gather outside City Hall 2night for 1 month memorial of Kendrick's collapse #kendrickhealth

stock exchange closed again today…even the mighty oak of commerce bends before john kendrick

Praying for you @MayorJKendrick from outside Bellevue Hospital. Hundreds of us are here waiting for good news!

Join us outside Gracie Mansion

Meet today in Times Square—will be biggest vigil yet #collectivemourning

At end of 6th week in Hospital, Drs are concerned about possible anemia, but hopes are high that he'll pull through. #kendrickupdate

Vigil outside Kendrick's home tonight #collectivemourning

waiting outside Bellevue for glimpse of the mayor. anyone see anything?

See you under the Brooklyn Bridge for concert honoring Kenrick #collectivemourning

Hear it first. Follow @TracyHols for #kendrickupdate

holy crap did u see the fire still blazing in central park?

Looking out my office window, police trying to stop the crowd outside city hall, looks like it might turn into another riot…

BREAKING NEWS: Crowds all over NYC grow bigger, NYPD may not be able to quell, Violence feared

Can't take the thought of NYC without Kendrick—bring your voice to the street #collectivemourning

if he's alive, why won't he speak to us #kendrickhealth

talk to us John! Tell us you're ok!

join us and pray for kendrick #collectivemourning

who could replace him #collectivemourning"

Scene Two

Saturday, August 29

(Morning. Outside Bellevue Hospital, DENISE *holds a press conference.)*

DENISE: Thank you all for coming out, especially in this heat. On behalf of the entire administration, I'd like to assure you that Mayor Kendrick and his family appreciate and value your concern in this difficult time. I do not, uh, at the moment have any updates on the Mayor's health. But I will certainly make you aware of any developments as they are made aware to, uh, to me. Rest assured, his condition is stable.

I do know, though, that the Mayor is anxious for the City to return to normal as soon as possible. While the peaceful vigils have certainly been acknowledged and your support is welcome, the time's come to return to work, for the City to go on as before.

Since the riot at City Hall following his collapse two months ago, the day he first came here to Bellevue, too often have peaceful demonstrations resulted in damage to property and to individuals. The fires at Gracie Mansion and the deaths under the Brooklyn Bridge are all regrettable and avoidable. And we hope, he hopes the city won't suffer any further tragedy, especially amidst the sancity of peace and prayer.

I know you're concerned, but despite the Mayor's illness, the administration is still functioning, we still have everything under control. Please be safe. Keep others safe. That's what Mayor Kendrick wants most. Thank you. *(She starts to head off.)* No questions today. Thanks. *(As she's walking off, she pulls out her phone, dials. She waits a moment, then:)* John, I hate that voice mail greeting. Remind me to tell someone to change it. But if you get this, call me, please. I need your help.

Scene Three

(That afternoon. TRACY *is at a table in Gracie Mansion on her computer, bored, scrolling through Twitter.* TODD *enters.)*

TODD: Where do women keep their hose?

TRACY: Like for gardening?

TODD: Yes, I'm bringing my mother a garden hose.

TRACY: Well, I didn't know. / You came in here without context, talking about hose?

TODD: But, I mean, common sense alone would have— It's like talking to Amelia Bedelia.

TRACY: Check her underwear drawer.

*(*TODD *stares at* TRACY.*)*

TRACY: Yeah, okay, I'll do it.
Todd, come here, look at this.

TODD: You gotta get off that thing. Our brains aren't wired for that many voices at once. You're gonna give yourself an aneurysm.

TRACY: Everytime we leave the house we've got to sneak out through the cellar, duck under an overcoat into a black car; can't go anywhere with crowds. We're living like Anne Frank. *(Tiny beat)* Yeah, I know. The second I said it I knew.

TODD: Get some writing done.

TRACY: How? Mother Superior's keeping your dad all cloistered up in that hospital. She won't let me talk to him. And you won't— …You know, so what else am I supposed to do but get sucked into the gaping chasm of populist expression. Come here, you'll like this.

*(*TODD *reluctantly slumps over to the computer. He reads and shakes his head.)*

TODD: This is absurd.

TRACY: No it's not! People love you.

TODD: They don't know me.

TRACY: They love your father and, don't get all, whatever, but you've got more of him in you than I think you'd like to admit. Plus, studies have shown that better looking people are more trustworthy. And you're a Twitter-certified dreamboat.

TODD: You're worse than my students on that thing.

TRACY: Okay, first of all, I am doing your mother's bidding, so...

TODD: Searching for my name on Twitter is my mother's bidding?

TRACY: Let's call it beyond the call of duty. But when there aren't any more health updates for me to pass along to my many followers...

TODD: Yeah, and how many is that now?

(TRACY *squints at the screen.*)

TRACY: Two-hundred thirty-nine thousand four-hundred and twelve.

TODD: That's a big number.

TRACY: Big? That's, like, almost the entire population of Saint Louis.

TODD: Congratulations?

TRACY: When you set out to be a journalist, what do you want? You want to reach people, to shine light into the world. At the Dispatch, I was a candle. Now I'm the freakin' moon.

TODD: But what happens when your source runs dry? When he's gone.

TRACY: I'm Tracy Holstein, girl reporter. I'll find another story. And nobody, like, ever unfollows anybody on Twitter, so it's a captive audience.
This is only a good thing, Todd. And I can do it from Saint Louis.

TODD: I miss it, don't you? The pace, the attitude.

TRACY: Yeah, definitely. Definitely. *(She turns back to her laptop and is immediately sucked back in.)*

TODD: My mother's waiting for the hose at the hospital, though, so if you could—

TRACY: Todd, if you want me to get off the computer, there's one very good way to distract me.

TODD: Right here, in the middle of the day?

TRACY: I said *good* way.

TODD: Tracy, I know what you're talking about and I'm not having this conversation again.

TRACY: We're in the City so I can write this book, right? I mean, yeah, to help your mother while he's in the hospital, but, since that first night, this book is why we stayed.

TODD: Yeah.

TRACY: Okay, so how am I supposed to write if I can't talk to the only guy who it's about?

TODD: My mother doesn't want anyone disturbing him.

TRACY: And are you on her side or mine? *(Beat)* Fine, then if you won't ask her to let me talk to him, at least let me write about, you know, about the one thing you won't let me write about. The thing that could be my Watergate. The thing that could win me, no big deal, a *Pulitzer*.

TODD: Absolutely not.

TRACY: Why are you defending him? This is the man who's destroyed your life. He poisoned your childhood with his career and he's poisoning your adulthood with guilt. Why protect him?

TODD: He's got a right to, you know, dignity.

TRACY: Dignity? He imprisoned hundreds of innocent people. *(Small beat)* When he told you he was targeting the homeless and throwing them in jail, it bothered you enough to drive you away from home for *eight years*, Todd. What's changed? Why, suddenly, is this a secret worth keeping?

TODD: I'm not trying to keep it secret. I'm trying to— If someone else uncovers this, fine. By all means, roll the presses. But *he* told me. He...I think he trusted me.

TRACY: What good's an evil man's trust? Why did he even tell you? He had to know how you'd react.

TODD: He told me he wanted me to understand why he did what he did. Maybe I wouldn't at first, he said, but maybe all I needed was the proper perspective. He was wrong, so I left.

TRACY: What perspective could justify the complete degradation of the social contract?

TODD: A leader's responsibility, according to John Kendrick, is to know what's best for those who follow. That's the onus, that's the job. People—I remember he told me this—people don't know what they want or what they need. They know what they like. And what they like is being inside during a thunderstorm. The danger being close enough to hear but remote enough to know they're safe. Governing, for him, was—is keeping the window closed, the roof from leaking. Because that's what they need.

TRACY: But he's wrong. You know he's wrong. You were so disgusted by it that you ran nine hundred miles away.

TODD: Of course I don't agree with what he's done. But I can't claim to know any better. If you write about this, tear his legacy apart and have nothing to supplant it with, what happens to a city that's come to rely on him? Even a rotting beam holds up a roof.

TRACY: Yeah, until it doesn't.

TODD: Do you want to see what happens if you destroy the only thing keeping this city together?

TRACY: In which of Orwell's nightmares is a city of mobs and riots and vigils "keeping it together?"

TODD: I only told you about all of this because you forced me to explain why I left.

TRACY: Yes, how dare I force you to be, you know, *honest*.

TODD: I told you in confidence. You promised me.

TRACY: I don't understand why you have any right to dictate the terms under which I do my work.

TODD: Well aside from the fact that you have zero evidence, zero leads and I'm your only source…Tracy, isn't my asking you enough?

(Beat. TRACY *turns back to her computer.*)

TODD: The pantyhose?

TRACY: Hmm. I was under the impresion dirty laundry was *your* specialty.

(TRACY *doesn't take her eyes off her computer.* TODD *exits.*)

Scene Four

(The same afternoon. DENISE, *anxious, sits in the waiting room outside* JOHN's *room at Bellevue Hospital. As* HELEN *enters,* DENISE *stands.*

DENISE: How's he doing?

HELEN: Are you asking or the press?

DENISE: Helen, I've been working for John for seven years. He's my friend.

HELEN: He's stable.

DENISE: Stable. The word of the year.

HELEN: Do you have a problem, Ms Powell?

DENISE: Why is it that I have to hear from your son's little girlfriend that he's going in for surgery, or that the cancer's progressed, or that he's switching medications? I've earned more than that.

HELEN: You've been invaluable to John. No one would argue otherwise.

DENISE: And yet here I stand, feet away from where he's dying, on the wrong side of the moat.

HELEN: Ms Powell, this must be very difficult for you. But the doctors don't think visitors would be good for his condition.

DENISE: So, he's hale enough to remain acting mayor but can't talk to me for five fucking minutes? The city—the citizens who elected him to office— everything's crumbling. All you're doing by letting that girl act as your family bullhorn is scaring them, riling them up.

HELEN: They have a right to be updated on his condition.

DENISE: Then let him tell them himself. Have him issue a statement, at least. I'm doing what I can, I've arranged for the Commissioner to call the National Guard if the situation escalates— I'm trying, Helen. But I'm not him. I... They need *him*.

HELEN: I can assure you, Ms Powell, the final thing on my husband's mind when at last his long struggle's complete will be the people of this city. Until then, I trust, as I hope you do, that he's aware how best to serve.

It's been two months, Ms Powell. I don't believe, and I know John doesn't believe, that you require hand-holding. So unless you've come up here expressly to harrass a dying man and his wife, I'd like to spend some time with my husband before he goes in for a C T scan this afternoon.

(Beat. DENISE doesn't move.)

DENISE: Helen, that's not why I... *(Small beat)* Oliver.

HELEN: Oliver. Yes, I've spoken to John about all that and he's made the appropriate phone calls.

DENISE: You promised me John would fix this weeks ago.

HELEN: I know what kind of pain you must be in, but what more can I do?

DENISE: For two months, I haven't heard a word from him, about him, nothing. Commissioner Stewart assured me that if he were taken before the panels he'd be held in the basement of the Manhattan Municipal Building next to City Hall, but the mouth breathers who run the floor won't let me past the security. Every day, I walk next door—right next door—and every day they turn me away. I'm the second most powerful person in this administration and I can't get him out

because of the simple, impossibly significant fact that
I'm not the *first*.

John is the only one allowed to give the order to release
him. And according to Manhattan Municipal's sub-
terranian trolls, he hasn't said boo.

So, I find myself asking for your help, once again
stranded on the wrong side of the moat.

HELEN: If I'm not mistaken, Ms Powell, weren't you the
party responsible for his incarceration to begin with?

DENISE: He was supposed to be— Yes. I informed the
guards that he might be attempting to access some
files in City Hall, but I also instructed them just to toss
him into a holding cell over night. A slap on the wrist.
That's all.

HELEN: A slap on the wrist.

DENISE: There would have been a scandal. I was
protecting him.

HELEN: John should be up soon. I should be there when
he's awake.

DENISE: *(Dryly)* Helen, I'm… *(Deep breath)* I'm begging
you for your help. This is me begging. Like it or not,
I'm begging. So…do what you want with that.

HELEN: Ms Powell, I don't—

DENISE: Yes, I do understand that this my fault. And
I feel…enough. I feel enough. But right now, Helen,
you of all people should…I'm scared I might lose my
husband. Please. Let me talk to John. Let me ask him
myself. Please.

HELEN: Ms Powell, the prospect of losing half of
yourself is one with which I'm far too well acquainted.
If a word from John would release your husband, of
course he wouldn't hesistate. But—and I hope you
don't interpret this question harshly—but, perhaps, is

there a chance, after the slap on the wrist, that Oliver simply decided not to come home?

(Small beat)

DENISE: Are you going to let me see Mayor Kendrick? Will I at least get to say goodbye?

HELEN: I understand how you must be feeling.

DENISE: You're about to sit beside your husband as he wakes. You have no fucking clue how I'm feeling. *(She exits.)*

Scene Five

Sunday, August 30

(The next day. TRACY *in an office in City Hall. Seated across from a large desk, she's typing on her phone.)*

*(*DENISE *enters.)*

DENISE: Didn't mean to keep you waiting so long. There was a little flare up with the vigil outside the Stock Exchange. No one was hurt but...

*(*TRACY *hasn't looked up from her phone.)*

DENISE: Ms Holstein?

*(*TRACY *holds up her finger—one second.* DENISE *doesn't like that.)*

TRACY: Sorry, sorry. Just heard from Helen that a scan taken yesterday showed that the cancer's appeared in his left lung.

DENISE: His lung, that's... Did she say how long they expect him to...?

TRACY: *(Still typing)* No. Yeah, it's terrible, really... *(She finishes.)* Done. Sorry. Hi. So nice to finally meet you. Hi.

DENISE: Thank you for coming in, Ms Holstein.

TRACY: I figured I'd have to interview you eventually for the book—I'm writing an authorized biography of the mayor, I don't know if you— Of course you do. Duh. No, but for the last couple months everything's been put on hold, so I couldn't make it down. And today, to get here, I needed a whole police escort. Thing's are... Dark times, you know. Dark times.

DENISE: Yes. Well.

TRACY: So, how can I help you?

DENISE: I hear great things about you.

TRACY: Yeah? From who?

DENISE: It's wonderful to see another powerful woman making her way in the political sphere.

TRACY: I always say "The glass ceiling ain't nothing but a skylight."

DENISE: Sure. Sure. Right, well, I've got a question. (This is hard for her.) Nothing enormous, but I was hoping I could prevail on you, one woman to, uh, to another.

TRACY: I don't know what I could possibly do for you, but yeah, shoot.

DENISE: About two months ago, my husband... He's been taken into custody.

TRACY: No shit. Wow, that's— What did he do?

DENISE: Nothing. Well, not nothing, but not anything really. It was a misunderstanding. The point being that I have been trying, for months, to ask John to make a call. Essentially, to help him get released. He's the only one who can give the word in this particular situation. But, as you're aware, Mrs Kendrick hasn't allowed me to see him.

TRACY: It's frustrating, isn't it? She's built this, like, impenetrable wall.

DENISE: I was wondering more about Todd.

TRACY: He's not exactly on the best terms with papa. Hasn't spoken to him since he went into the hospital.

DENISE: Which is why I'm coming to you. I was hoping, given how much we have…in common, that you might consider seeing if Todd would ask on my behalf.

TRACY: First of all, thank you for thinking to ask me. Second of all, I don't know how you're coping. That's…I can't even imagine. But, I don't know. His father's a sensitive subject.

DENISE: If you could ask, it would be very helpful. Ms Holstein, my husband's freedom is at stake.

TRACY: I guess, maybe I could *ask*, but, sorry, why did you say he was he arrested? In case Todd asks. Or John.

DENISE: He was— He was doing research in City Hall, accidentally wandered into a section that was marked classified, got nabbed by a guard.

TRACY: And he's been in jail for two months? That's insane. How is that possible?

DENISE: Well, there may have been some unfounded, drastically mistaken suspicion that he had something to do with the Derelict threat.

TRACY: He went before the panels.

DENISE: I would imagine so, yes.

TRACY: And without any evidence, without a trial, without a modicum of jurisprudence, he was thrown in jail. That's amazing! Not amazing, obviously, but you're saying this happens, sometimes, which is terrible. But it happens?

DENISE: He's innocent, Ms Holstein. With Todd's help, with your help maybe we could get him out.

TRACY: Has this happened before? That an innocent man or woman's been put in prison without trial, the administration essentially, just, you know, spitting on the Constitution? *(Beat)* I don't see why I couldn't ask Todd. But it'd be helpful to know, for when I talk to him, has this happened before?

DENISE: I think...I believe it's possible that it has.

TRACY: Sorry, just to clarify, you're saying it's happened before? So I can tell Todd.

DENISE: Yes.

(TRACY leans back, suppresses her excitement.)

TRACY: People need to know about this.

DENISE: Not now. Now people need to go back to normal, to their lives.

TRACY: I know you've been trying to calm everyone down, but, like, maybe this information would help.

DENISE: I really think it's best if I decide when this sort of information's revealed. This is, after all, my job.

TRACY: And I'd never pretend to be able to tell you how to do it.
But maybe seeing the faults of Kendrick's administration would allow them to let him go. Maybe it'd help.

DENISE: What about maybe not working them up with news about the Mayor's white blood cells every day? Maybe *that* would help.

TRACY: Do you see something wrong with what I've been doing on Twitter? I'm informing the people. They have a right to be informed.

DENISE: And we have six well-bred recent graduates of the finest J-schools in the country whose sole task is manning this office's Twitter feed, and who are paid minimum wage to do it.

TRACY: So there's no place for journalists not on the City Hall payroll?

DENISE: I'm not— Ms Holstein, despite this room of trained employees, despite the myriad of other outlets this administration has to reach the press, you have taken it upon yourself to provide near-constant revelations about the health of the man who it is my job to advise and protect. Furthermore—

TRACY: Well, I didn't exactly—

DENISE: Furthermore, with each incessant update, you're managing to rile up the entire Internet-accesible population of this city. I'm asking you to leave Informing the People to this office, to me.

TRACY: So, what, you're censoring me? Silencing the press? Yeah, voters just *love* violations of the first amendment.

DENISE: All I'm asking is that you consider the implications of your actions. Ms Holstein, I trust I don't have to explain to you that what you put out into the world has an effect. And right now, that effect is forcing frightened people to hear, on a daily and excruciating basis, the details of the decay of the man they worship.

TRACY: So you want me to stop?

DENISE: You're egging them on. You're in over your head and you don't know what you're doing.

TRACY: They don't have to listen.

DENISE: This is America so you're allowed to be as stupid as you'd damn well like, but please don't play naïve. (*Beat. She realizes she's overstepped.*) I didn't mean that. I'm tired, all the time, I'm scared, I…I'm sorry.

(*Small beat*)

TRACY: Those six underpaid staffers you've got manning your Twitter account. Do they follow me?

DENISE: I don't…I don't know. Ms Holstein—

TRACY: Tell them to start.

Scene Six

(*The same day.* HELEN *is seated outside* JOHN's *hospital room, reading a book.* TODD *approaches.*)

HELEN: He's asleep.

TODD: How's he doing?

HELEN: When he wakes up, why don't you ask him? He's just on the other side of this wall.

TODD: How are you doing?

HELEN: Me? I don't know. Sad. Very…sad. I'm tired. The cushions on these chairs are a lousy replacement for the posturepedic.

TODD: I can't believe you've been here this long. Go home for a night.

HELEN: And if something happens, you'll be with him? (*Small beat*) I'll stay.

TODD: So, he's—he's stable?

HELEN: Is Tracy asking?

TODD: No, but I'm just, I'm curious; how much time, do you think, does he have left?

HELEN: He's stable. Today.

TODD: And then—?

HELEN: That's life, Toddie. The "and then."

(*Beat*)

TODD: It's a cruel joke, isn't it? Human beings, we're not built with the capacity to comprehend eternity. And yet it's the only thing every single one of us will have to contend with. (*Small beat*) If people, if they find out about what kind of a leader Dad was, what do you think's going to happen?

HELEN: They know what kind of leader he is.

TODD: But if they learned about what he's done, everything he's done...

HELEN: Who can say. Right now, they're grieving.

TODD: But after he dies, I mean, later, once the dust has settled. Don't people have the right to know?

HELEN: Afterwards, Toddie, someone's going to have to put the pieces back together. If the entire city's lost all faith in its leadership, well, that's going to make it a heck of a lot more difficult.
Why the sudden interest?

TODD: I don't know. Just...thinking.

HELEN: You came all the way down here to think? Go on, Toddie. Go in.

TODD: And say what?

HELEN: It doesn't matter. Anything. Tell him what he wants to hear.

TODD: Which is what, Mother?

HELEN: Apologize.

TODD: Apologize!? For what?

HELEN: For Saint Louis. For the last eight years, the last two months. You're his son.

TODD: Are you out of your mind?

HELEN: You left. Because of what? Because you didn't like the way he does his job? He's your father. What has he ever done to you, Toddie?

TODD: What has he done to *them*?

HELEN: What exactly has he done? Those Derelicts he's put in prison? Is their life not more livable than it was when they were on the street? They have food, they have shelter.

TODD: What about freedom?

HELEN: What about freedom? They had their shot at freedom, and they were plenty free to squander it. The great, necessary myth of Democracy is that freedom and happiness are mutually reliant.

TODD: Yeah, well, they have neither.

HELEN: Those poor, helpless people are better off. And what's more, this city is.

TODD: But at the very least, his constituents have the right to know what he's done, don't they? Let them judge him for themselves.

HELEN: You think they'd understand? Or care? If the well-being of most can come at the sacrifice of a few, isn't that the choice society must make? Your father's achieved what he has by creating a unified society, where the majority remains content, unafraid. Unified, Toddie, by a common enemy.

TODD: That's all shadow boxing! They're a hollow threat!

HELEN: Until now.

TODD: Until now.

HELEN: They returned when they must.

TODD: Talk about timing. After twelve years of warnings, they finally resurface. Just in time to stir up fear, create some mayhem before he dies.

HELEN: Toddie, how many threats do you think City Hall receives from the Derelicts each and every day?

TODD: I have no idea.

HELEN: More than this one.

TODD: So what makes this one dangerous?

(Small beat)

HELEN: If I answer, will I have to wait eight years to see you again?

TODD: I'd like to know. What makes this threat so serious?

(Small beat)

HELEN: It's serious because I asked him to take it seriously.

TODD: You asked.

HELEN: This city's far too great a challenge for one man, however great, to carry on his own.

TODD: But the letter... Why?

HELEN: In times like these, it's best to remind the city why it needs its heart.

TODD: There's no threat?

HELEN: There's always a threat. And your father's always kept us safe. If he's about to leave, the city should see he's keeping us safe until the end.

TODD: You lied. To keep them scared, you lied.

HELEN: You're thinking of this moment, Toddie, of today. Think about tomorrow. We're etching stone on the monolith of human history, in the shadow of which

most of us are scattered pebbles. The greatest gift a
wife can give her husband is a place in history.
A great man deserves a great monument.

TODD: You did all this for his legacy?

HELEN: His. Yours. Mine. But, no. I did this, as I've
done everything for the last twelve years, for this city.
They need to mourn him. And then they'll need a new
leader. A powerful leader, possessing a trust forged in
the fire of tribulation, a leader who proves, from the
start, he can overcome.

TODD: The city's on the brink of bursting into flames
because of this. Because of you.

HELEN: For twelve years he's held the city together.
Despite how it may seem to you, this won't be its
downfall.

TODD: You're wrong. You're...you're toxic.

HELEN: I'm curious, Toddie, what is it you think you
know that he doesn't? What perspective do you claim
that gives you the right to vilify?

TODD: I'm a good man.

HELEN: Are you?

TODD: Yes. I'm a decent person. Which is more than I
can say for him.

HELEN: What makes you good?

TODD: I don't know know, I am. I don't—manipulate
and lie. I'm a—I'm a good man. I'm a school teacher.
I've dedicated my life to broadening minds. I give to
charity...when I can. I keep my head down. I let other
people live their lives.

HELEN: That doesn't make you good. That makes you
insignificant.

TODD: I'm a good man, Mother.

HELEN: What have you done to make this world a better place for other people, other than stay out of their way? That's easy. That's cheating. Being responsible for others, wrestling with how your actions, how what you do affects other people, that's hard. And that's politics.

TODD: I never wanted to be a politician! / That's not—

HELEN: More vitally, that's life. It's only the adolescent or the fool who believes that when he sticks his hand in an inkwell, that ink's not going to get on everything he touches. You're good at estrangement. At blindness. You're selfish, Toddie, and you've always been.

TODD: I'm not selfish! I stayed here because you asked for my help! I'm helping *you*!

HELEN: And what did that cost you? Grow up. Selflessness isn't giving to others. It's sacrificing of yourself. What have you ever had to give up? What have you ever sacrificed? I've given my life and my husband to this city.

TODD: I'm a good man!

HELEN: Toddie, you haven't earned the right to call yourself a man.
Sacrifice something, little boy. Throw something that you care about on the altar and watch it die. Maybe then we can have this conversation.

(HELEN *walks away, leaving* TODD *alone outside his father's room.*)

Scene Seven

(That night. DENISE, in her home, dials her phone, waits, then:)

DENISE: *(On the phone)* John, really got to change that outgoing greeting. It is beyond condescending. Hi, it's me.

(The following tweets are either projected or are read by TRACY or are presented to the audience in some other clever fashion.)

> *Hello, followers looking for updates on the Mayor's health. Stay tuned for big revelation. Retweet!*

DENISE: *(On the phone)* I heard about the, uh, about your lung and I feel... I'm sorry. But I'm out of options. I don't know what to do.

> *Get big news here BEFORE you hear it on the news tomorrow. YOU WON'T WANT TO MISS THIS #kendrickbombshell*

(TODD, in Gracie Mansion, frantically grabs his phone and dials. He glances repeatedly at the computer screen before him.)

TODD: *(Hanging up the phone)* God DAMN it. *(He dials again.)*

DENISE: *(On the phone)* If you get this message, or any of my messages, please, John, call me back. It would be nice to hear— Shit. Someone's on the other line. *(She switches over the call.)*

> *#kendrickbombshell (1/4) Has come to this reporter's attention that for the last twelve years, Mayor Kendrick has wrongfully imprisoned*

TODD: *(On the phone)* Tracy, where are you? Get off the computer right now! Stop this, Tracy. Please. Just… / Call me back! NOW! *(Hangs up)* Shit. *(He dials again.)*

> *(2/4) hundreds of innocent homeless men and women to avoid the costly prospect of reintroducing / them to society.*

DENISE: *(On the phone, concurrent with below)* Whoa whoa whoa Grubman, slow down… Take a deep breath, and then speak… Hey, hey! I can't understand you if you talk that fast.

TODD: *(On the phone, concurrent with above)* Tracy! Get off the computer now. Sign off now. Where the hell did you go? Tracy. Where are you? You have to stop! *(He hangs up.)* / Goddammit!

> *(3/4) He has done this, he would claim, to avoid the crime, violence, drugs and repeated offenses these people 'cause'*

DENISE: *(On the phone)* At City Hall?

TODD: *(Feverishly texting. Under his breath)* Goddamn it, Tracy…

DENISE: *(On the phone)* What do you mean "attack"?

(TODD dials again.)

DENISE: *(On the phone, concurrent with below)* Slow down, Grubman, it's gonna be— …A bus? A city bus? …Holy shit. Holy fucking shit. I've got to…I've gotta go, Grubman…I said shut your fat fucking face, I have to go!

TODD: *(On the phone, concurrent with above and below)*
Goddamn it, Tracy! STOP! STOP NOW! ANSWER
YOUR PHONE AND GET OFF THE FUCKING
INTERNET NOW! You have no idea what you're
doing. You're making a huge mistake. COME HOME
NOW! *(He hangs up the phone)*

(Concurrent with above:)

(4/4) You heard it hear first, from @TracyHols—More info tomorrow #kendrickbombshell

We can make it right. You can make it right! Begin by realizing Kendrick is fallible. He's wrong. Go home and rest! A new day tomorrow

(Alone, after the above have finished:)

Goodnight, NYC. Thanks for listening. Sweet dreams.

Scene Eight

Monday, August 31

*(Extremely early the next morning. TRACY stands, wearing
a backpack and smoking a cigarette on a street corner.)*

(TODD appears several feet away.)

TODD: What the hell is wrong with you?

(TRACY jumps back, startled.)

TRACY: Jesus, Todd. You scared the crap out of—

(TODD rushes over and throws his arms around TRACY.)

TRACY: What are you doing? Why aren't you at home?
It's like— What time is it?

TODD: Five.

TRACY: What are you doing on the street at five in the morning?

TODD: I've been running all over the Upper East Side looking for you. Why isn't your phone on? Why the hell wasn't your phone on!?

TRACY: I turned it off. I needed to unplug.

TODD: I didn't know if you were— Where you were or— Your phone was off. Never do that again! Ever!

TRACY: Turn my phone off?

TODD: Never!

TRACY: I needed some time. Some silence.

TODD: Where. Were you.

TRACY: Nowhere. I was walking around the—

TODD: When you sent those tweets, where were you?

(Small beat)

TRACY: You saw? Shit, Todd, I wanted to tell you before you— Listen, I know you're mad at me. You have every, every right to be mad at me. Though I will point out that until two months ago you had lied about just about, like, everything. But Todd—

TODD: Enough, Tracy.

TRACY: At least let me explain. I'm sorry, I am, but I got confirmation, a second source. Denise Powell. So it's not on you. Something like this, it was bound to come out eventually—

TODD: Tracy, stop—

TRACY: And you have to see what a huge opportunity this would be for me. / This is, like, the scoop to end all scoops.

TODD: Just shut up, Tracy. SHUT UP!

(Silence)

TRACY: Excuse me.

TODD: Do you have any idea what's happening?

TRACY: Did you just tell me to shut up?

TODD: Tracy, you've got to get out of here. Off the streets.

TRACY: Todd. What's going on? Is this about your Dad? He didn't— Oh, Todd, Is it over?

TODD: I told you not to do this. Didn't I…I warned you! People do not like being told they're worshipping a false idol. A decade and a half of building trust and then a crackpot takes to Twitter—

TRACY: Oh, I'm a *crackpot* now?

TODD: What do you expect them to do?

TRACY: I don't know! Think. Realize that he's not a god. That he's made mistakes, terrible mistakes. Maybe realize he's not worth, you know, all this.

TODD: Yeah, well, Tracy, that's not what happened.

TRACY: Todd…

TODD: There was a riot. Or not a riot, a, uh, a crowd that got out of hand down by City Hall. It's worse than any of the other— There was a fire, there's been major structural damage. It's still burning. The entire area, it's— Every building in and around City Hall Park is either ashes or on its way there.

TRACY: *(Concurrent with below)* Oh my god, Todd. Todd, that's terrifying. I don't even—

TODD: *(Concurrent with above)* There're thousands of people in the, there's—The building's coming down, Tracy. And according to the news… They're blaming you. Eyewitnesses at the protest claim this started when the crowd read your…Jesus, Tracy, your photo's all over.

TRACY: I don't…Todd, I don't understand—

TODD: They're scared.

TRACY: But they're always scared.

TODD: Yeah, but when they're terrified and angry, they look up at that big photo in Times Square. Now that John Kendrick's not there— You lit the match, Tracy.

TRACY: They don't believe me? They think I'm lying?

TODD: Why does it matter? As far as they're concerned, what you said is sedition. If they can find you, Tracy, I don't know what they'll do. You're not safe.

TRACY: But I can prove it. We'll ask Denise Powell. She'll know where there's proof. Todd, my reputation as a journalist is on the line.

TODD: Tracy, you caused damage! Actual, tangible damage! Not to your career. Not to someone's feelings. To people. People are dying, Tracy.

TRACY: I'm sorry. I didn't know…

TODD: You need to grow up. What you do, what you say has consequences. *You* did this.

TRACY: Todd…Todd, I'm sorry. I'm sorry, I didn't mean to—

TODD: Tracy, you can't be here. / The whole city's looking for you.

TRACY: It's going to be all right, isn't it? It'll be okay? Jesus Christ. Todd, I'm scared. I'm scared and… You know this wasn't my fault, don't you? I didn't do this on purpose.

TODD: We'll talk about it later.

TRACY: Oh my god. Oh my god.

TODD: Let's get inside.

TRACY: Wait. Todd. Wait.

TODD: Later.

TRACY: No, Todd, wait. I shouldn't have—I was wrong,
I made a mistake. But you can fix this.

TODD: Tracy…

TRACY: People trust you, I've seen it. You're his son.
If you tell them, they'll listen. If you tell them I'm not
lying, if you tell them the truth, they'll listen. Just, tell
them I'm not lying. Tell them it's true. And then we'll
go back, Todd. We'll leave and we'll go straight home.
And we won't come back. We'll leave, Todd, please.
Please talk to them.
Talk to them tomorrow. Tell them and they'll listen.
Todd…
Todd…
…Todd…

Scene Nine

(Later that morning. A recording of JOHN's *voice plays over
darkness.)*

JOHN: You have reached the office of Mayor John
Kendrick. I'm not in at the moment, but there's nothing
I love more than hearing from you, you fine New
Yorkers. So leave a message.

(A beep)

*(*DENISE *appears, leaving a message.)*

DENISE: Man, John, that outgoing message. I know it
was my idea but…
Hi. It's me. Denise.
Denise Powell.
I didn't know who else to… Look, I know you're not
going to check this voice mail. You've got other things
on your plate, I'm sure. Lymphoma, for one.

And by the time you got down to City Hall, there'd be nothing left to check.

I don't know why I'm doing this. This is stupid. This is so fucking stupid. *(She exhales.)* Well, John, turns out I don't have a lot of people I can call. And if I did, they'd just *talk*, so—

You're a fucking asshole, you know that? You really are. I've been working for you for, what, seven years? And you couldn't have maybe mentioned any of the messed up shit you were doing?

So, John, I just wanted to call this morning to tell you to fuck off and die.

And also…for not telling me…thank you, John.

I don't know if they're letting you watch the news up at Bellevue, or if you're awake, or… Thought I'd fill you in.

Last night, John, last night someone in one of those crowds high-jacked an abandoned city bus. He, uh, he didn't love what some people were saying about you. Didn't want to believe it could be true. So he drove that bus into the ground floor of City Hall. Of course the crowd went wild, John. How could they not? They got hold of cabs and cars. Trucks, even. And they drove them one by one through the first story windows, leaving a heap of them right there in the foyer. Then someone tossed a torn up rag and a jug of gasoline through the front door. The building… The building is demolished, John. The whole block… They're afraid, John. Isn't that what you wanted?

All night, I was praying all night that they unlocked that basement cell before they ran. Before the flames took down the building just across the street. But I'm not anymore. No, I know… Now, I can't help it, I try, but I just keep praying he wasn't alone. *(Small beat)*

If you had said anything, done anything… *(Small beat)*
I have to call the National Guard. Get them to send
helicopters or boats or…
No. John. This isn't why I called. It's not. You know
why I called? I called to tell you:
I quit.
I can't do this anymore.
I can't pretend to—

VOICE: This message has exceeded the maximum
length allowed. If you would like to leave a message,
please dial this number again.

(A dial tone)

Scene Ten

(The same afternoon. HELEN *and* TODD *are seated in the
hallway outside* JOHN's *room in Bellevue.)*

HELEN: The cameras are waiting.

TODD: How's he doing? I know they'll ask.

HELEN: It's not long, Toddie. He sleeps more than he's
awake, and even then, he's barely lucid.

TODD: Oh.
Do you think once he goes, all the madness out there is
going to stop?

HELEN: I do. The job then is the rebuilding.

TODD: What's going to stop them from keeping on like
this until they've destroyed the entire city?

HELEN: Someone will tell them not to.

TODD: It's that easy.

HELEN: These citizens, they're like children. They like
to believe they have independence, but when they're
sick and hurt and lost, they need to know someone's

in control. Now, in order to rebuild, they need the strength that comes with unrelenting certainty.

TODD: But without Dad, who?

HELEN: I don't know. Someone who's willing to give himself to their well being. Someone they trust.

TODD: A steady hand in the midst of a crisis.

HELEN: *(With a smile)* You've been a great help these last few months. I will always be grateful that you came when I called. Know that.
Do you know what you're going to say?

TODD: No fucking clue.
I know, I know, idiot's fucking wheelhouse.

HELEN: *(With a smile)* The silence has gone on long enough. They need to hear from this family.

TODD: I can't do this.

HELEN: You can. Everything will be fine.

TODD: How can you say that?

HELEN: Because you're more like your father than you'd like to admit. And he's always been able to see what's best.

TODD: You know, I think maybe I'm more like you.

HELEN: Maybe.

TODD: I don't want to do this.

HELEN: No one else can.

TODD: I'm scared.

HELEN: I wish I could take all this fear, all this pain from you and burden my own heart. But, today, you're the only one who can decide what they need to hear. And decision, Todd, is the most refined art of sacrifice. It is. With every decision you make, you murder possibility and... Possibility is why we breathe, why we rise in the morning, why we cling to life until it's torn from our white-knuckle grasp. And yet, we give up a piece of it every time we make a choice. It's hard at first. But it gets easier, Todd, this sacrifice. It gets easier.

(TRACY *enters wearing enormous black sunglasses, her head wrapped in a black scarf. She's incongnito.*)

TRACY: Hi.

TODD: You shouldn't be here.

TRACY: You wanted me to sit at the hotel and watch on TV like everybody else? I thought you knew me better than that. I wanted to be with you.

HELEN: Ms Holstein.

TRACY: Hello, Helen.
How are— (*She swallows, nervous*) How have you been?

(HELEN *is about to say something. She decides against it.*)

HELEN: (*To* TODD) I'm going to go tell them you're on your way.

(HELEN *approaches and runs her fingers through* TODD's *hair along his temple. She holds the back of his head.*)

HELEN: It gets easier, Todd. I promise. (*She kisses his forehead, then exits.*)

TRACY: How're you feeling? You nervous? (*She adjusts his collar.*) Okay, so I've been thinking about it, and I think there's a way we can explain what your father did and still keep your mother in the clear. If you want to. I mean, I don't know how you're leaning. Just in case you don't want to, you know, throw her under the proverbial... Let me see your speech.

TODD: I haven't written it. I don't know what I'm going to say.

TRACY: You haven't— That's fine. Give me, like, two minutes. I think I can get the salient points out fairly succinctly. Do you have a pen?

TODD: I don't know what I'm going to say.

TRACY: You're going to tell them I didn't make all this up. You're going to tell them what your father's done and that he explained it all to you. I don't think Denise Powell's itching to do me any favors, so looks like you're the only source I got. I need you here.

TODD: Once I tell them, there's no undoing. His legacy, everything he worked for throughout his entire life will be...dust.

TRACY: There are innocent people in prison. If you know and say nothing you might as well have sentenced them yourself.

(Small beat)

TODD: Do you think I'm a good man?

TRACY: You? The best.

TODD: Why?

TRACY: Because you're kind. You're considerate. You're respectful.

TODD: But do I do good?

TRACY: You don't do bad. And that's better than most. What you're doing now, helping me, helping those innocent men and women, letting the world know who your father really is, that's doing good. You doing good.
And then it's over. It's all over. We can get on a flight tomorrow. Go back to Saint Louis, to our quiet lives, our stupid neighbors, our duck-shaped mailbox. School starts in a week, and then...
Todd, we're so close. And I am so ready to brag to all our friends about how the man who saved me—yes,

quiet, indecisive Todd Nevelson—is the man I got to marry. *(She hold his face in her hands, smiles and examines him.)* Look at you. Even at the gates of hell, kiddo, you are one hell of an enigma. *(She kisses him again and steps back.)* I'll see you when you're done.

(TODD walks off. TRACY, alone, runs her fingers along the band of her ring and closes her eyes.)

Scene Eleven

(That afternoon. Outside Bellevue, TODD holds a press conference, nervously checking a few prepared notes.)

TODD: Thank you all for coming. As you are all aware by now, last night a series of horrific events occurred at City Hall and the, uh, the surrounding areas. I understand that the National Guard, in addition to sending a force to, you know, to suppress the riots, is going to be sending boats and helicopters to begin evacuating some of the affected neighborhoods. They should— Or, I guess, they're supposed to arrive at Battery Park tomorrow morning at the, uh, the latest. I'm, I'm sure an official in the administration will have more details for you soon. *(He puts down the notes.)* I also…I feel I must address the, uh, the circumstances, which may have led to last night's events. Some of you may have heard some information regarding my father, Mayor John Kendrick. It's my responsibility to inform you that there's no truth to these rumors. They are merely that: rumors. Hearsay. And my father urges you, I urge you, to begin the process of rebuilding, of getting this city back to normal.
I cannot say I understand all of what my father's done in his time as mayor of this city. But I know that when my father passes on, it will be with the assurance that he's done what's best for the people of New York. I

know this is true. And today, I'm asking you to trust in me.

I won't be taking questions. Thank you.

Scene Twelve

Tuesday, September 1

(The following morning. JOHN is asleep in his armchair, his back to the audience. HELEN speaks to him softly.)

HELEN: Sunrise. September.

The heat's broken at last, dear heart. The knowing breeze of impending fall is whistling through the city streets. You slept right through the end, yet here we are.

When you awake, you'll see a testament, a testimonial, a tribute. A city changed as if by magic in the night. A great work, our work, at last complete. September First.

When this city's historians recall this day, the day eight million built a pyramid for one great man, what date could be more fitting than September First. Your birthday.

When you awake I'll tell you all about last night. The homage to our wonder. I'll tell you how your son has paved the road on which you'll make your final exit. I'll tell you how a single rag and a single bottle set Fifth Avenue aflame. And how the fire's been creeping up the Empire State Building all night long, only now, at day break, reaching the top floors at last. A torch, like Lady Liberty finally coming home to dry land. You can see the fire burning through the windows, climbing up the building, snaking up the floors, wrapping the skyscraper in smoke like a vine.

And when you wake I'll tell you of the eight people, eight men in mourning who weaved their cars through

the throngs to Manhattan's edge. How spread out
around the periphery, they each drove out to the
center of a bridge, one for each of Manhattan's eight
stone and metal tethers. I'll tell you how one by the
one, the bridges collapsed into the rivers, releasing us.
Releasing you at last.

And when you're ready, you can rise and look out the
window here at the street where the city erects for us
a tumulus, a burial mound. Built of iron, dirt, flame,
glass, cement, pain, steel, concrete, reverence. Our
work is done, dear heart.

For now, just sleep. All this can wait till you're awake.
(She rises, kisses him on the forehead.) Happy birthday,
John.

Scene Thirteen

*(The same morning. Battery Park. DENISE looks out over
the river toward Liberty Island. She holds a large manilla
envelope and a purse. TRACY approaches with her suitcase.
She's not wearing her ring.)*

TRACY: She's still standing.

DENISE: I'm sorry?

TRACY: Lady Liberty. She's still standing. The whole
world's coming to an end and she hasn't blinked. I'm
jealous.

DENISE: The world isn't coming to an end, Ms Holstein.
Only New York.

TRACY: Yeah, well, sometimes when you're here, it's
hard to tell the difference.
You got a cigarette?

DENISE: Sorry, I quit.

TRACY: Yeah, me too.

(DENISE *reaches into her purse and takes out a pack of American Spirits. She hands one to* TRACY.)

TRACY: And you've got my brand. Thank you. *(She lights the cigarette.)*

DENISE: They're Oliver's.

TRACY: Oliver's your...

DENISE: Husband. He's my husband.

TRACY: Oh.

DENISE: I don't know what you're after, Ms Holstein, if you were coming over here to apologize or beg for my forgiveness or hear a big fucking "I told you so" or what. But I'm not accepting regret at the moment. Try again some other time.

TRACY: Really, I never meant for any of this to happen.

DENISE: I know. Please leave.

(Beat. TRACY *turns to look behind her.)*

TRACY: You see those high-rise buildings over there? Behind them. You can see the smoke coming off the Empire State Building. It's not out yet. Still burning. *(Small beat)* What do you think's gonna happen to this place?

DENISE: Ms Holstein, I have no fucking idea.

TRACY: Well, somebody's got to clean it up.

DENISE: I say let it burn. Let the whole thing burn forever.

TRACY: Aren't you the one who's responsible for, you know...putting humpty dumpty together again?

DENISE: Not anymore. Once the National Guard arrives, I'm done. I just want to be sure people get out of here safely. That's all.

TRACY: You quit? *(Small beat)* The helicopters are late.

DENISE: *(Checking her watch)* Not yet.

(Small beat)

TRACY: How long do you think it's going to keep on burning?

DENISE: Ms Holstein, I'm not in the mood to— You want absolution? Fine. It's not your fault. If it wasn't you it would have been someone else. You're off the hook. This is how it had to end. This was the only way. Turns out Oliver was...
So, there you go. You didn't light the match, you just tossed it on the pire.

(DENISE turns away from TRACY.)

TRACY: I do feel guilty, Ms Powell. But that's not...I'm sorry.

DENISE: I forgive you. Why won't you just let me be alone?

(For the first time, we see a glimpse of terror and sadness from TRACY. It's almost instantly tamped down.)

TRACY: Because I'm afraid. And I don't know want to be al— ...I don't know anybody else here.
I'm sorry to bother you, Ms Powell.

(Small beat. TRACY turns and then:)

DENISE: I saw Todd's press conference yesterday.

TRACY: Yeah.

(DENISE looks over her shoulder at the burning city. As she speaks, she may even forget she's talking to TRACY at all.)

DENISE: All this for one man. One son of a bitch.
Most people die without fanfare, without acknowledgement that they were ever alive to begin with. Most people die in a basement, in the dark... alone.
My husband wrote a book, did I tell you that? *The*

Chronicle of the City of New York. It was thousands of pages long, just immense. He made me promise I wouldn't read it until it was finished. But of course I read the whole thing. All four-thousand eight-hundred and sixteen pages. Some mornings, before he got up or at night after he went to sleep, I'd sneak into his office and I'd read what he had written.

TRACY: And?

DENISE: Oh, it was brilliant. He saw this city in a way that… He saw that this city had a life, was a living breathing creature. And that all living things die. He looked at it from above. He knew.
All I wanted was for him to stop writing, come back down to earth. And I prayed that he never would. *(She runs her finger along the edge of the manilla envelope.)* I found this in his desk under the pack of cigarettes. I thought he quit.

TRACY: You think you know someone. Every atom, every cell. And then you realize… People, I've noticed, are remarkably surprising.

(Small beat)

DENISE: *(Looking at her watch)* Okay, now they're late.

TRACY: Denise, if there's anything I can—

DENISE: Let's not. Okay?

TRACY: Well, thanks for the smoke.
Goodbye, Ms Powell.

DENISE: *(Nodding to* TRACY*)* Ms Holstein.

TRACY *(Turning to look at the skyline)* Good riddance.

*(*TRACY *takes her suitcase and walks away.* DENISE *pauses for a moment before opening the envelope.)*

DENISE: *(Reading)* "Dear Sir or Madam,

Several months ago, you rejected out of hand a book,
a history of New York City. At long last, it appears my
subject may have provided me with the conclusion it
seemed I'd never find. And in the spirit of completion,
I give you a memento of a fallen Viking.
Enclosed please find the final chapters of this
unfounded fiction, *The Chronicle of the City of New York.*
I submit them to you, you charlatans, you philistines,
at last, for publication. Once you've wiped the ashes
from your eyes, perhaps you'll deem them a suitable
end to an unsuitable feat.
Sincerely Yours, Oliver Judd."

(DENISE *smiles and turns to the final page.*)

(OLIVER *appears and recites.*)

OLIVER: Someday, free of her moorings, she will drift
into the sea. The bridges all snap their tethers and
release her. A barge on which the whole of humanity
has turned its eyes, Manhattan, free of her chains,
floats through the bay.
Past Brooklyn, off the shore of Long Island, she drifts.
The Subway burrows through dirt like an earthworm,
stopping occasionally to let riders glimpse out the
windows, now portholes to the murky sea.

(JOHN *appears in his armchair in the hospital. He is gaunt,
his yellow skin drawn tight across his bony frame. Wires
and I V tubes extend from his body. His breaths are labored.
*HELEN *sits alongside him, stroking his hair. She is all
tenderness, all devotion.*)

OLIVER: Beyond the tip of Montauk and up past the
Cape and soon, Manhattan sails through open waters,
the choppy Atlantic tumbling off the edge of the
horizon at every compass point. Unobstructed sunlight
bounces off the great glass windows of Wall Street,
off the stately stone of the Museums and the Concert
Halls, off the hot dog vendors' carts and the row boat

hulls in Central Park, off the rusted beams of the elevated lines and the sweeping copper rooftops of old New York.

(TRACY *reenters and looks out over the water at the Statue of Liberty. In the distance, we hear the sounds of approaching helicopters. She takes a drag of her cigarette and exhales.)*

OLIVER: And the people rejoice for the fresh air and the water and the sun. And their city.

(TODD *enters* JOHN's *bedroom.)*

(DENISE *looks out over the bay, lost in thought.)*

OLIVER: And then, every evening, the city joins together and prepares to unplug every lamp, turn out every bulb, dim every headlight, and extinguish every candle.

(HELEN *rises and, after pressing her hand to* TODD's *cheek, she leaves the room.)*

(*The lights go out on* TRACY *and* DENISE, *both staring across the calm waters of the open harbor.)*

OLIVER: A hush falls over the city.

(TODD *and* JOHN *stare at each other for a long time.)*

OLIVER: And quietly…so quietly…the clocks in the highest towers across New York strike midnight. And the city goes dark.

(TODD *opens his mouth to speak, unsure of what to say.)*

OLIVER: It happens all at once. In a snap. *(He snaps.)*

(Blackout)

OLIVER: *(In darkness)* And for once, you can see the stars.

END OF PLAY

www.ingramcontent.com/pod-product-compliance
Lightning Source LLC
Chambersburg PA
CBHW052112090426
42741CB00009B/1776